Partnerships For Classroom Learning

Partnerships For Classroom Learning

From reading buddies to pen pals to the community and the world beyond

SUZANNE GIRARD

KATHLENE R. WILLING

Heinemann
Portsmouth, NH

Pembroke Publishers Limited
Markham, Ontario

© 1996 Suzanne Girard and Kathlene R. Willing

Pembroke Publishers Limited
538 Hood Road
Markham, Ontario L3R 3K9

Published in the United States of America by
Heinemann
A division of Reed Elsevier Inc.
361 Hanover Street, Portsmouth, NH 03801-3912
ISBN (U.S.) 0-435-07230-7

Canadian Cataloguing in Publication Data

Girard, Suzanne, 1950-
    Partnerships for classroom learning

Includes bibliographic references and index.
ISBN 1-55138-067-6

1. Education, Elementary — Activity programs.
I. Willing, Kathlene, 1937- . II. Title.

LB1555.G57 1996   372.1   C96-931058-7

US Cataloguing in Publication data available from the Library of
Congress.

A catalogue record for this book is available from the British Library.
Published in the U.K. by
Drake Educational Associates
St. Fagan's Road, Fairwater, Cardiff CF5 3A3

Design: John Zehethofer
Cover Photography: Ajay Photographics
Typesetting: Jay Tee Graphics Ltd.

Printed and bound in Canada
9 8 7 6 5 4 3 2 1

Contents

Acknowledgments

The majority of the programs described in this book were developed and implemented by the authors over the past ten years in cooperation with other teachers in Canada and abroad. Additional contributions were generously made by other educators.

We thank our former intermediate and primary students at Montcrest School in Toronto, Ontario, who participated in buddy programs and enjoyed the benefits of mixed-grade interaction. Two kindred spirits, Dorena Kelly and Bernadette Power at West Royalty School in West Royalty, Prince Edward Island, kindly shared their unique buddy program with all of us.

The contributions of the following educators are very much appreciated: Lorna Engwall, principal at Lincoln Elementary School in Sterling, Illinois; Bonnie Berry, teacher at Archie Stouffer Elementary School in Minden, Ontario; and David Mowat, teacher at Haliburton Highlands Secondary School in Haliburton, Ontario. Their innovative partner programs provide a wealth of ideas for others wishing to make community connections.

Olga Butch at Unionville Public School in Unionville, Ontario, and Audrey Lum at Meadowridge School in Maple Ridge, British Columbia, and their students have had successful pen pal programs over the years. These experienced teachers have demonstrated their commitment to creating a variety of opportunities for authentic reading and writing experiences in their language arts curriculum.

We are grateful to Ronjel Smith-Stuart, formerly of Port Maria Primary School in St. Mary, Jamaica, and Lucia Emilaire at Babonneau Infant School in Babonneau, St. Lucia, along with their students who participated in twinning programs over many years. They were enthusiastic, diligent, and creative in reaching out to their Canadian twinned classes. Resources supplied through the Canadian Teachers' Federation's former School Twinning Program served as excellent guidelines.

We commend the project led by Alicia Garces and Eureta Bynoe at Earlscourt Junior Public School, Toronto, Ontario, and Barbara Howard at Cuthbert Moore Primary School in St. George, Barbados.

We are indebted to Susan Barter at The Bishop Strachan School in Toronto, Ontario, who brought her expertise to bear by reading the manuscript and making pedagogical and practical suggestions.

The administrators of these participating schools are applauded for lending support to their staff, enabling them to add a special dimension to their classes' learning environments by going beyond their classroom walls.

And finally, many thanks to Abe Kabayama who kept us supplied with iced tea and lunches during the warm summer days while writing. His caring support was appreciated.

Introduction

July 10

Well, I finally did it. I bit the bullet and hooked up that second-hand modem I bought last fall. Not as complicated as I thought, and it's actually working! Guess I just needed a reason to put it into action. The computers-in-education course provided the incentive, and the instructor's electronic bulletin board opened a whole new world. What a concept — you have a problem or need some ideas about teaching. You leave a message in a conference that interests you and then some teacher you don't know from Adam responds to your message and helps you out. Talk about hands across the water! I signed up for the "electronic village," which is an electronic network of teachers — and links up students as well.

August 14

Came across an interesting posting while cruising the "electronic village" this morning. Someone in the Primary Conference posted an invitation to join a Flat Stanley Project. Never heard of Flat Stanley, but my curiosity won't let me pass it up. Also, communicating with teachers across the United States and Canada sounded great. So "Yeah," I said, "count me in."

August 16

Wow, e-mail is swift! Got a reply already and looks like I'm committed. The organizer of the project is gathering names and addresses of other teachers and will be sending a packet by snail mail in a few weeks. Hope I can convince the Grade Two teachers to get involved in this project.

August 30

Spent some frustrating time in school today trying to get organized. The summer renovations look super, but the lab won't be ready on time — furniture not placed according to our diagram, computers not hooked up, strange file cabinet in the middle of the room. Decided not to give myself an ulcer so came home early and discovered good news waiting for me — the *Flat Stanley* packet arrived and looks great. Twenty-four teachers signed up — Michigan, Hawaii, Texas, Alaska, California, New Brunswick, and Ontario. The package includes the names of several Grade Two and Grade Three teachers, their school and e-mail addresses, and some project ideas. Now I've got to find the book. Reminder: check school library for **Flat Stanley** by Jeff Brown.

September 6

I'm on a roll — found **Flat Stanley** in our library and both Grade Two and Grade Three teachers are interested. Not a hard sell at all! Gave each of the teachers copies of the package to look over. The Grade Two teachers want to start immediately — reading the book on the first day. Then they'll have the kids make their own "flat people" to mail out. My part is to have the kids write their letters on computer when they finally come to the lab. Oh, yes, it's still in limbo! Now to see what the Grade Three teacher will come up with.

October 2

What excitement! We received our first Flat Stanley from Texas and the kids were highly motivated to get to their letters. Will send copies of this home for sharing with parents along with a cover letter. Would you believe September zipped right on by and the lab is just now up and running? The Twos came down today and finally started their letters. We saved their first efforts and they will continue in their next sessions. Their flat people are ready — some really imaginative ones, such as Flat Sonic, Flat Dragon, and Flat Mom! Can't wait to get these letters finished, sent out, and receive the replies. Helped the Grade Three teacher introduce a Flat Stanley that came in from New Brunswick today. The class plans to take him along when they go to the CN Tower.

The Global Community

Today's students will be members of a global community in the twenty-first century. It will be a time of challenge with continuing social and technological changes. To prepare for this unknown world, students need to develop a clear sense of their own identities and their role within their home community. More important, they must become aware of students in other communities around the world. To deepen their understanding of both commonality and diversity, they must exchange their thoughts, hopes, and concerns with others. Partnerships within schools and between classrooms provide opportunities for such exchanges.

Partnerships for Classroom Learning describes how we and many teachers have built partnerships for our students and classrooms that in some measure address these issues. It has been written at a time when education is responding to change by promoting adaptation in schools, teachers, and curriculum. Learning environments are taking on a sense of community, providing the space for group learning and leaving room for informal communications. Teachers are becoming risk takers. Drawing on their lives outside the classroom, they have a global view, depend upon their communication skills, and appreciate the role of technology. As facilitators, they value teaching techniques that are co-operative, collaborative, and consultative. Curriculum is also being modified to meet changing needs and environments. With learning no longer confined within the walls of the classroom, the community is viewed as a vital component of curriculum — a critical resource upon which teachers and classrooms can draw.

Developing Multiple Literacies

One principal curriculum goal of today's classroom is to create learning experiences in which students gain the knowledge, skills, and values necessary for life-long learning. Meaningful real-life situations that emphasize independent inquiry, problem solving, and new technologies are being brought into traditional subject areas.

Through learning programs that stress the connections among ideas, people, and things, students develop their concepts of change, interaction, and interdependence, enabling them to form a holistic view of life that includes multiculturalism, as well as issues of social responsibility and respect for the diversity of the human community.

Information literacy means the ability to use technology at all points in the curriculum, and partnership programs provide many opportunities for students to develop in this domain. As they use technology to gather information, prepare their documents, and share their communications, technology becomes a natural and even essential part of their lives.

11

Today's students are expected to effectively acquire, critically evaluate, and thoughtfully communicate information from ever-changing human, material, and physical resources. Through their work with buddies, with others in the community, or with pen pals or twinned classrooms, students come to value the richness of these resources and learn how and when to draw on them.

Developing a World View

Partnerships for Classroom Learning addresses the need to educate students with a global perspective by presenting programs that are suited to changing schools, teachers, and curriculum. To meet current educational goals, many teachers are now looking beyond their classrooms to establish communication connections for their students. As shown in the following diagram, these connections can be close at hand and readily available in a teacher's own school or community. But, without leaving the classroom, teachers and students can also reach out to other parts of their country and the world. The concentric circles of this diagram identify only the geographical limits of some possible contacts; programs such as these can be implemented in any order, and more than one can be put in place at a time.

Reaching Out

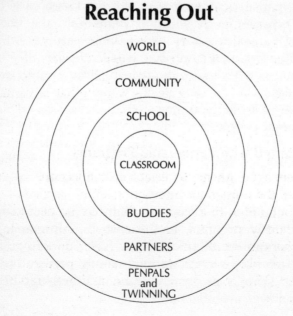

The diagram shows the expanding horizon possible for teachers and their classrooms. Reaching out from the classroom into the school setting, teachers can set up buddy programs with other classes. Extending further, they can make connections within their community and establish community partner programs. Ultimately, they can forge links with classrooms around the world through pen pal programs and twinning programs.

Growing by Reaching Out

Students who participate in buddy programs have the opportunity to develop their own identities while they get to know others of different ages in the familiar setting of their own school. They communicate orally, work co-operatively, and share resources.

Community partner programs put students in touch with supportive teenagers and adults in a variety of settings. These partnerships promote social skills, as well as oral and written communication. Their activities involve sharing resources within the school and the community.

Pen pal and twinning programs match individual students and/or classes to bring worlds together through information exchanges. With direct access to knowledge about their own and other cultures, students develop greater confidence in their own cultural and racial identities.

All participants in partnership programs enjoy significant benefits. In general, these real-life experiences inspire students to pay closer attention to current events, develop new vocabulary, enhance their communication skills, appreciate other points of view, and think critically. Many other advantages become apparent as the programs unfold.

Getting Started with Partnership Programs

For teachers who intend to establish connections beyond the confines of the classroom, contacting other teachers with the same outlook is the first step. All that may be necessary to establish a buddy program, for instance, is informal talk with other teachers in the school. Because fewer opportunities exist to explore possible contacts for community partners, pen pals, and twinning programs, some planning and preparation may be worthwhile.

Teacher Information Sheet

I am interested in setting up an educational contact that goes beyond my classroom walls. This contact could take different forms, such as individual pen pals, cyberpals, an Internet project, class or school twinning, or a community connection. The following information may help you determine whether my class would be a good match for yours. Please contact me for additional information if you are interested. I would need similar information from you if you are.

Teacher name _____

Grade _____ Number of students in class_____

School _____

    Address _____

    Telephone _____

    Fax _____

    E-Mail _____

Subjects/ Themes Taught _____

_____

_____

Special Interests _____

_____

_____

Project Ideas _____

_____

_____

_____

_____

During the course of the school year, most teachers find themselves at meetings, workshops, courses, and conferences, all of which are ideal forums to meet other educators. Gathering information about potential classroom partners can be facilitated through the use of a **Teacher Information Sheet**.

After completing the **Teacher Information Sheet** with information about their own interests and classes, teachers can copy and distribute the sheet whenever professional exchanges take place. They can mail, fax, or e-mail the sheet to others who have expressed common interests in journals and magazines or on the Internet.

Implementing Partnership Programs

After contacts have been made and planning is under way, graphic organizers, such as the **Time Line Planner** on pages 16 to 18, are useful for visualizing details for the year. Information is recorded along the time line so that the sequence and co-ordination of individual tasks becomes apparent. With so many other school activities demanding attention, time lines make it easier to assign priorities to program tasks and to create reliable schedules, and they can become records of the program for the year. You will find an example of a completed time line in each chapter.

Involving Families

An important component of any partnership program is family involvement. No matter what kind of program is being implemented, students will have items to take home and share with their families. When this validation of school initiatives occurs, children are more motivated to continue their efforts. Letters are a prime way to establish communication links between the class and the home — starting at the beginning of the school year with an introductory letter and continuing throughout the year with updates to keep the families informed. A final letter at the end of the year summarizes and assesses the program and thanks families for their interest and support.

Newsletters can serve the same purpose by introducing the program and then highlighting achievements and special events along the way using text, photographs, and the children's art.

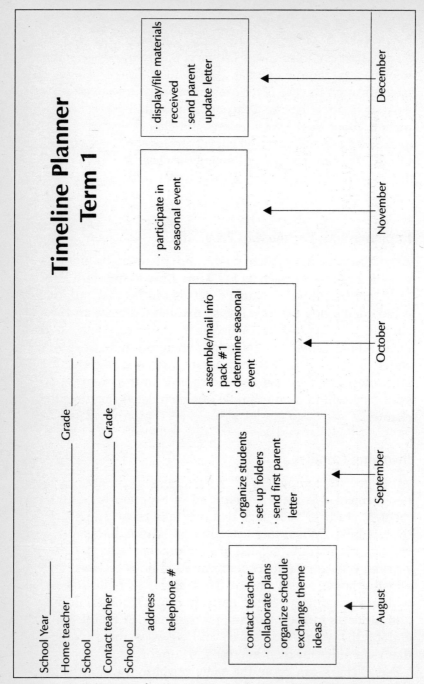

Timeline Planner
Term 1

School Year _____ Grade _____

Home teacher _____

School _____

Contact teacher _____ Grade _____

School _____

address _____

telephone # _____

August
- contact teacher
- collaborate plans
- organize schedule
- exchange theme ideas

September
- organize students
- set up folders
- send first parent letter

October
- assemble/mail info pack #1
- determine seasonal event

November
- participate in seasonal event

December
- display/file materials received
- send parent update letter

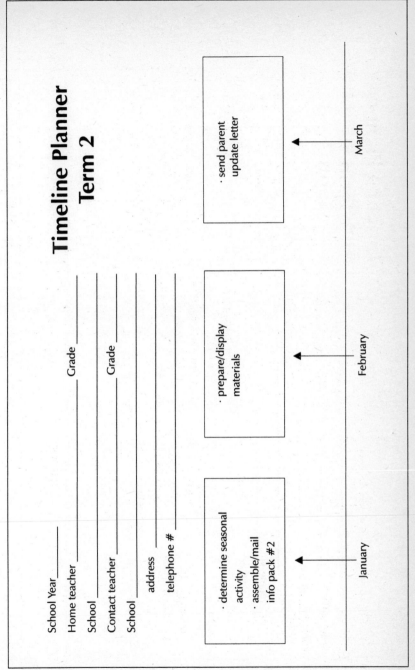

Timeline Planner
Term 2

School Year _____

Home teacher _____ Grade _____

School _____

Contact teacher _____ Grade _____

School _____

address _____

telephone # _____

- determine seasonal activity
- assemble/mail info pack #2

- prepare/display materials

- send parent update letter

January   February   March

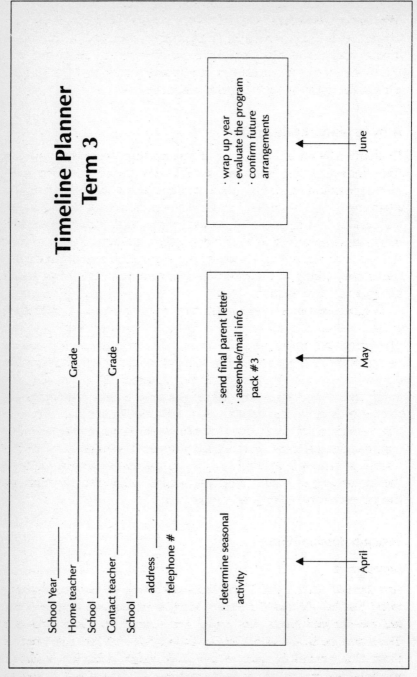

Timeline Planner
Term 3

School Year _____
Home teacher _____
School _____ Grade _____
Contact teacher _____ Grade _____
School _____
address _____
telephone # _____

- determine seasonal activity

April

- send final parent letter
- assemble/mail info pack #3

May

- wrap up year
- evaluate the program
- confirm future arrangements

June

Personal contacts are yet another means to involve families. Whenever there are special events, trips, and displays concerned with the partnership program, families can be invited to attend and perhaps to participate. During the course of the year there are many opportunities for family members to volunteer time and expertise, or to donate resources.

A Note about Evaluation

Evaluation is an integral part of partnership programs and can take many forms, such as pencil and paper, performance, personal communication, and student collections. During the planning stage, teachers generally have an idea of the desirable outcomes in the areas of knowledge, skills, and attitudes. Regardless of the type of program and the activities in which the students are engaged, teachers can recognize gains their students are making in their knowledge, communication and social skills, and other abilities.

Teachers assess student work and involvement in partnership programs in the same ways that they assess learning and programming within the classroom. The process and products of connections beyond the classroom are highly appropriate for both student and teacher portfolios. Checklists, response journals, and observation are other possible tools. Teachers may decide to involve their students in self-assessment and combine the results with their own efforts. Comments from families, community partners, and other interested parties may prove useful. It can be beneficial to have assessment plans in place at the beginning of year. Progress can be monitored throughout the program and at the end of the year.

Teacher Journal Entry

November 14

Saw the Flat Stanley from New Brunswick sitting in morning assembly today! Just love the way Flat Stanley inveigles his way into the curriculum and into the kids' hearts. This project is a natural! The Grade Twos and Threes are even incorporating Flat Stanley into field trips. And now I can get Grade One involved by tying in with their science. A teacher in Hawaii mentioned that her students do weather readings all year and that it would be nice to share data with a school in a northern climate. Well... Grade Ones study ice and snow in January as part of their science, and so Flat Stanley can stretch in another direction. The Grade One teachers have agreed — their students can take temperature readings, note the weather for a bulletin board graph in the hall, and then exchange readings with Hawaii by e-mail. We'll graph them in different colors. Hey, I wonder if we could...

1 / Buddy Programs

June 13

Boy, there wasn't a dry eye in the house, especially mine. I can still see shy little Amanda as the Grade Ones took their turns presenting flowers to their reading buddies at graduation. Kyle didn't know what to do at first when she whispered to him in front of the audience. When he bent down to listen, she gave him a big hug. I could tell by his red face that he wasn't expecting it, but he handled it like a pro. Would you believe he hugged her back, and they left the stage hand-in-hand? Who would have imagined in September that tough ol' Kyle would turn out to be such a softy? Not me!

When Edward approached me last fall about doing reading buddies with his Grade Eights, I must admit that I was hesitant. Some of his students worried me when I thought of their playground behavior. Especially Kyle's. I knew that much of his acting out resulted from his poor language skills, and I wondered how this would rub off on my impressionable little ones. How could he possibly relate to a beginning reader? On the other hand, I wanted my kids to have as many chances to read as possible — so I crossed my fingers, took a chance, and said yes!

I almost backed out when Edward matched his boisterous Kyle with my timid Amanda. Although I agreed that she was a good student, I thought someone more nurturing would be better. How wrong I was. Once they got to know each other, Amanda looked forward to their weekly reading sessions, and Kyle even chatted with her in the school yard.

It was at the Halloween party that things really jelled. Imagine, those Grade Eights decorating their classroom and taking care of all the refreshments. Edward said they spent their recesses planning it. My kids were thrilled — playing pin-the-tail-on-the-black-cat, bobbing for apples, and partying for an hour is their idea of a good time. Kyle endeared himself to Amanda when he emerged from the tub of water with that apple in his mouth and his hair dripping wet. She burst out laughing and so did I.

Edward and I were hoping that our classes would get along. We noticed more and more that they were. It was really something to see the reading buddies tucked into the corners of the hallways and perched on the stairs totally absorbed in their picture books and oblivious to the world around them. Edward was amazed that Kyle kept Amanda busy by asking her what she thought would happen before turning almost every page!

I remember the look on Amanda's face the day Kyle turned up with her favorite book. Apparently she'd mentioned it a while back, and he tracked it down at the library. That means he must have his own library card now. Looking back, am I ever glad I took the risk. Getting to know each other did both of them a lot of good.

Buddy Partnerships

Buddy partnerships connect students in the same school. Buddies are paired and meet regularly as partners in learning. Matching students provides a supportive environment and adds a stimulating dimension to the classroom. Pairing across grades or divisions allows children of different ages to interact. Extending their range of social interaction helps buddies — especially those without younger or older siblings — relate to different age groups.

Particularly effective pairing occurs when primary and intermediate students are matched. Older students provide models of appropriate behavior for younger ones and gain in self-confidence through opportunities to be nurturing and patient. They develop listening and reading skills and experience a variety of activities. Their knowledge about child development grows, and they begin to understand what younger children are capable of doing. In helping younger children, a metacognitive process takes place — analyzing the task at hand, thinking about the sequence of instructions, and then evaluating their effectiveness as the helper. Attitudes to learning can undergo changes when students see themselves in their younger buddies.

Younger students, with their fresh perspective and openness to learning, generate enthusiasm in their older partners. Like their older counterparts, younger students make gains in listening and reading skills. The sharing of experiences and the extra attention provided by the older partner can improve self-concept and accelerate learning.

Buddy programs are reciprocal in nature. In their role as facilitators, older students gain leadership experience by guiding and supporting their partners' inquisitive nature. Regardless of their ages, students are challenged by appropriate responsibilities and benefit from one another's extra attention and enthusiasm.

Buddy sessions can be focussed on any subject across the curriculum — reading, writing, math, science, or social studies — and provide a convenient time for students to practise new skills they have learned. Whatever the subject area, students develop their listening, speaking, and social skills.

Reaching Out

Since buddy programs are set up within the school, making arrangements with another teacher to have two classes work together is relatively simple. In the course of their day, teachers have many opportunities to get to know one another. They see each other in the staff room, sit on committees, and lead extra-curricular activities. As they chat informally, they discover they have compatible teaching styles and complementary curriculums. This may lead to working collaboratively on joint ventures that may be planned or that may happen spontaneously. It can also lead to establishing a buddy program.

Organizational Planning

After two teachers agree to implement a buddy program, they can begin their planning. As they work together, they should give some thought to the following:

- program focus
- program duration
- frequency of sessions
- matching students
- preparing students for the program
- involving families
- fostering collaboration

Determining Program Focus

Buddy programs can be set up in any subject area, or in more than one area at a time. Common cross-curricular themes, such as space, rain forests, or fairy tales, can define a program. Short-term projects dealing with, for example, structures, magnets, pioneers, or composers, are also suitable for buddy programs.

Determining Program Duration and Frequency

In the initial planning, participating teachers can decide how long the program will last and how frequently buddies will get together. Programs that last the entire year tend to be subject-oriented, whereas short-term ones are generally project-focussed. Available convenient times will depend on individual timetables and will determine how often the classes can get together and the length of the sessions. With year-long programs, continuity can usually be maintained with sessions every two weeks. Short-term projects that are task-oriented may require more frequent sessions. Once settled, the dates and times can be blocked out on the school calendar for the duration of the program.

Matching Students

The matching process is very important, as a strong bond is likely to occur between the paired students. Teachers often use their students' personalities and academic levels as the criteria for matching. Outgoing students might be matched with shy ones; less confident students might be paired with supportive partners. Students may be matched with their own or the opposite sex. When class sizes are different or some students are particularly demanding, buddies can be doubled up, and threesomes can be used to accommodate extra students. Such personalized groupings benefit all students involved.

Nevertheless, mismatches can occur, and some flexibility may be necessary to ensure that the buddy program is fair to everyone concerned. Teachers need to pay close attention to the wide range of interpersonal nuances that exist in their classes and have conflict resolution strategies in place to ensure successful experiences for all.

Preparing Students for the Program

Before they embark on a buddy program, students need to know what to do and what to expect of their roles. Regardless of their ages, students should be supplied with communication tools and reading strategies and not left to their own devices. In mini-training sessions, they can be coached to work together and resolve conflicts. Familiarizing them with teaching techniques, as found in the **Tutoring Tips** in this chapter, will help them become effective guides and coaches. Behavioral guidelines, such as those in the **Behavior Tips** in this chapter, will point the way toward ensuring effective buddy relationships.

After the buddies have been matched up, interest inventories, possibly designed by the students themselves, can be used to introduce buddies to each other and to establish rapport.

Involving Families

As with any classroom program, it is worthwhile to advise families about the program and its progress. In an initial letter, teachers may wish to present an outline of how the program will work, their expectations for it, and how it will benefit their students. Subsequent notes can present updates and may contain photographs or other items of interest. Newsletters may also be useful for highlighting special successes and events. At the end of the program, students may wish to celebrate their partnerships by hosting an open house for their families.

Fostering Collaboration

Buddy programs present advantages to teachers as well as to students, offering the opportunity for teachers to work collaboratively with one another. Each teacher will bring different experiences and expertise to the initial planning, and such planning can invigorate the teaching practice of both. Planning, monitoring, and evaluating the buddy program will be shared responsibilities, as will teaching and administrative tasks such as writing letters, making telephone calls, and keeping records. Buddy programs invite team teaching, with one teacher introducing and concluding a lesson and the other presenting the content and engaging the buddies in the activity.

Curriculum Planning

After teachers have their organizational planning in place, they can consider the following:

- subject area focus
- specific projects
- program extensions
- program assessment

Tutoring Tips

We were all young once, so remember that your buddies are just learning new skills as you did. Here are ten tips for successful tutoring:

- Be patient, and allow enough time for your buddy to complete the task.

- Allow time for your buddy to think before giving an answer.

- Preview books by examining covers and illustrations.

- Break instructions down into small steps.

- Listen carefully when your buddy reads.

- Ask open-ended questions.

- Help by pointing out and explaining tasks.

- Ask questions and make suggestions when your buddy is stumped.

- Use reading strategies (context clues, predict, imagery).

- Check which materials or equipment are necessary for tasks.

Behavior Tips

Here are ten tips to make your time together enjoyable:

- Say hello at the beginning of each session.

- Smile and be pleasant throughout the session.

- Be firm, fair, and consistent.

- Pay attention.

- Treat each other the way you want to be treated.

- Use a friendly voice.

- Share and take turns.

- Give sincere praise and encouragement.

- Seek help with conflicts when all else fails.

- Say good-bye and thank you at the end of each session.

A year-long buddy program usually focusses on one of the subject areas of the curriculum. Reading, a pivotal skill, has connections in all subject areas and is a frequent starting point for such programs. When students are paired for the purpose of reading, they select books from the library, classroom, or their personal collections to read to their buddies. Teachers can also present a range of reading materials suitable for class themes or individual projects, or that meet personal interests.

Within a buddy program total reading time is increased, and younger children have a non-threatening environment in which to develop their oral reading skills. Invariably, they benefit from the extra attention, listening opportunities, and reading time. Their enthusiasm is well received by older students who offer guidance and support their oral reading. Buddies develop a sense of responsibility and ownership by choosing relevant and appropriate materials for their sessions.

In another area of the curriculum, younger students can be paired with older ones to work with Sign-Out Science (SOS) bags. These open-ended science activities in bags contain all the necessary equipment and materials to carry out simple experiments.

Once the bags have been made by teachers or students, they can be signed out by science buddies. Students select bags they think their partners might like or ones that they favor and want to share. Given a purpose for choosing a bag, both partners benefit from the decision making process.

As they formulate and test hypotheses and conclusions, students develop science concepts, reinforce their science skills, and extend their scientific knowledge and their critical thinking skills. Open-ended questions at the end of the experiments encourage additional experimentation and further research and provide opportunities to apply what has been learned.

Conducting the SOS activities provides science buddies with a means of manipulating and questioning aspects of their environment. Students bring their own level of comprehension, skill in following directions, interpretation of their observations, and divergent thinking to the task. For the most part, older students have higher skill levels in all of these areas; however, opportunities remain for students to interact in a complementary fashion. For example, the younger child may be more task oriented and keep the older partner on track. (For more information about these activities, see *Sign Out Science*, 1993.)

During the year, students are also involved in a variety of activities that are cross-curricular in nature. For example, buddies meeting to explore math concepts could represent the geometric shapes in an art activity or compose number stories in a language arts activity. A buddy program with a social studies focus might lead students into exploring games from around the world. Music and physical education could then be used to convey the chants and the movements of the games.

A technology component can also be built into buddy programs. Buddies can work together at the computer, whether in the classroom, lab, or library resource centre. They can investigate software together, design invitations, create posters, or type letters. In these ways, they discover practical applications for their new communication and technological skills.

Specific Projects

Specific projects are characterized by a short time frame, perhaps a month or a term, and structured activities. They can be either part of a year-long program or separate and distinct units on their own. As buddies work together on a project, they meet frequently for specific purposes, such as writing stories, using the computer, playing math games, making science observations, drawing maps, constructing models, or producing books. As students work together in novel situations such as these, their learning and interaction are often intense.

Some buddy projects provide an additional subject area focus within an overall program and lend themselves to teaming with more than one classroom during the year. For example, a Grade Three class could work with Grade Eight students on a language arts project in the fall, with Grade Five students on a science project in the winter, and with Kindergarten students on a visual arts assignment in the spring.

An important part of collaborative curriculum planning is in generating buddy project ideas. The two classroom teachers can initiate the planning and then draw upon the expertise and resources of others in the school, such as the teacher-librarian. A visual organizer, such as the **Buddy Project Web** in this chapter, can be used to integrate projects across the curriculum in the areas of language arts, mathematics, the arts, science, social studies, and physical education/health. The activities in the sample web are suitable for elementary students from mixed divisions.

Sample Buddy Project Web

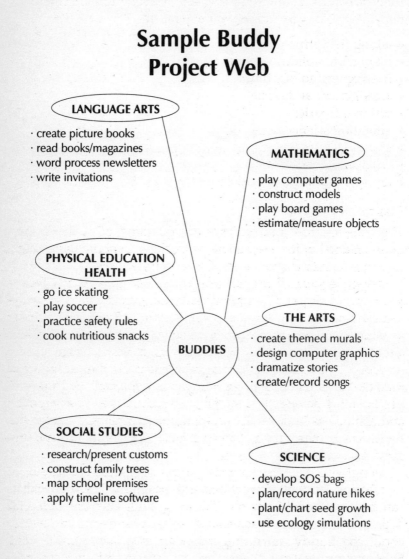

LANGUAGE ARTS
· create picture books
· read books/magazines
· word process newsletters
· write invitations

MATHEMATICS
· play computer games
· construct models
· play board games
· estimate/measure objects

PHYSICAL EDUCATION HEALTH
· go ice skating
· play soccer
· practice safety rules
· cook nutritious snacks

BUDDIES

THE ARTS
· create themed murals
· design computer graphics
· dramatize stories
· create/record songs

SOCIAL STUDIES
· research/present customs
· construct family trees
· map school premises
· apply timeline software

SCIENCE
· develop SOS bags
· plan/record nature hikes
· plant/chart seed growth
· use ecology simulations

Program Extensions

Activities to extend buddy programs are limited only by the amount of time and other resources available to carry them out. Activities such as the following may be part of the initial planning process or can happen spontaneously:

- taking field trips
- organizing holiday events
- hosting technology days
- creating arts and crafts
- visiting libraries
- attending science fairs
- playing games/sports
- celebrating end-of-year
- exchanging summer postcards

Program Assessment

The collaboration that enriches the planning of a buddy program extends to its assessment, as teachers combine their efforts to evaluate their students, projects, and programs.

Response journals are an effective component of any buddy program or project. Describing response journals in his book of the same name, Les Parsons says they are "a notebook or folder in which students record their personal reactions to, questions about, and reflections on what they read, view, listen to, and discuss . . . and then reflect on how and why they respond as they do." In the buddy program, response journals become simple tracking devices for students to record their participation and feelings as buddies. In addition, the journals are a reference for teachers monitoring their students' development and progress for evaluation purposes.

Along with response journals, simple checklists are useful for monitoring student interactions and progress. These checklists can be developed from the **Tutoring Tips** and the **Behavior Tips** in this chapter. Teachers can assess a student's knowledge about the buddy, nurturing behavior, and task commitment. Students can evaluate themselves by posing and answering reflective questions, such as the following:

- Did I co-operate with my buddy?
- Did I listen carefully to my buddy read?

- Did I make sure we got the job done to the best of our abilities?

A Sample Time Line — A Year at a Glance

When implementing a buddy program, it is useful for both teachers to have a time line, progressing from August to June, for reference throughout the year. Blank **Time Line Planners** can be found on pages 16, 17, and 18. Dates of scheduled meetings can be located on the line, and organizational and curriculum planning details can be added in sequence, providing, for example, reminders to make home contacts or initiate special projects. This graphic organizer can also be used as a checklist or to record up-to-date notes.

The sample time line in this chapter sets out a buddy program for a Grade One and a Grade Six class. The Grade One teacher had already done a variety of buddy programs during his ten years at the school. This year, while the library was being renovated and access to the books was limited, he was seeking another way to increase his students' reading time. The Grade Six teacher, starting his first year, offered to collaborate with the Grade One teacher. As part of the technology component of his curriculum, he wanted his students to use software called HyperCard to create stacks of different screens with text, graphics, and sound. He realized the Grade One stories would lend themselves to that format. The Grade Ones would provide the text, and his students would be responsible for the illustrations and the recorded reading of the stories. The younger students would then experience their own stories as talking books on computer.

August

At the end of the summer holiday, the two teachers got together to plan their buddy program. Because the Grade Ones needed to share books and read their own stories, and the Grade Six students needed an authentic purpose to create HyperCard stacks on computer, the teachers determined that the focus for the year would be reading, with a special short-term technology project to be included.

The teachers scheduled regular buddy sessions every two weeks during language arts time. In the spring, project sessions

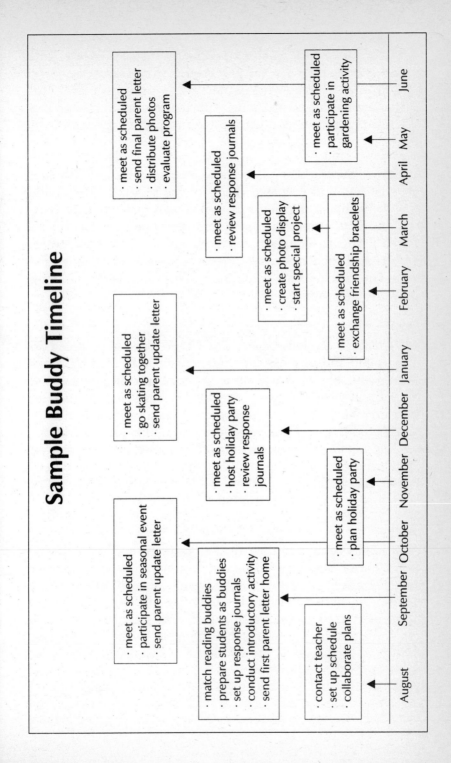

Sample Buddy Timeline

August
· contact teacher
· set up schedule
· collaborate plans

September / October
· match reading buddies
· prepare students as buddies
· set up response journals
· conduct introductory activity
· send first parent letter home

· meet as scheduled
· participate in seasonal event
· send parent update letter

November
· meet as scheduled
· plan holiday party

December
· meet as scheduled
· host holiday party
· review response journals

January
· meet as scheduled
· go skating together
· send parent update letter

February
· meet as scheduled
· exchange friendship bracelets

· meet as scheduled
· create photo display
· start special project

March
· meet as scheduled
· review response journals

April / May
· meet as scheduled
· participate in gardening activity

June
· meet as scheduled
· send final parent letter
· distribute photos
· evaluate program

in the computer lab would be added once a week. The teachers decided that parent contacts would be handled by the Grade One teacher and the special project would be taken care of by the Grade Six teacher. They would share the responsibility for special events and for working with the teacher librarian. This was noted on time lines posted in their respective classrooms.

September

As soon as the teachers got to know their students a little better, they matched and prepared them for the program. The Grade Sixes were shown tutoring tips to use with their younger partners, and both classes discussed and developed written behavior tips. Students set up separate notebooks as response journals and attached their tips inside the front covers. Meanwhile, the Grade One teacher sent home their first parent letter outlining the buddy program.

October

The scheduled sessions began. The Grade Ones were doing an autumn unit and so the older students helped by finding books in the public library that were appropriate for their work. The Grade Sixes gleaned ideas from their reading and decided to create an autumn trail in a nearby park. They took their buddies on a guided tour and enjoyed roasted pumpkin seeds and popcorn that the Grade Ones had made for a snack. Their response journals indicated that the joint venture was a success. A parent update letter highlighting the hike was sent home at the end of the month. A sample update letter is on page 35.

November

The students continued their reading sessions and, in addition, used some of their time to plan a holiday party and write in their response journals. At the beginning of each session, they worked on decorations and entertainment for their party. Buddy pairs used greeting card software on the classroom computers to create invitations for their families. During the last few minutes of each session, the Grade Ones dictated their journal entries for their buddies to record.

October 28

Dear Parents,

We would like to take this opportunity to bring you up-to-date on the buddy program we introduced to you last month.

Your child has been meeting regularly with a buddy every other week. They are enjoying the opportunity to read and listen to one another.

We would like to encourage the older students to continue borrowing books from the public library and the younger ones to keep bringing books from home. In this way we can be sure of having a variety of books on hand throughout the year, in addition to our class collections.

Our major highlight of October was the nature hike in Greenland Park that the Grade Sixes organized for their buddies. They looked for signs of autumn, identified trees, collected leaves, and recognized wildlife.

November will find us planning a special event for December, which we hope you will be able to attend. Your child will be bringing more information home about it soon.

Sincerely,

Bob P. and Prakash D.

December

The excitement level rose during the last few buddy sessions as the students finished preparations for their party. On the appointed day, they decorated the larger classroom and set up tables to serve cookies and drinks. The buddies acted as hosts and greeted their families and other staff members when they arrived. Refreshments were served after the guests had enjoyed the skits and songs performed by the buddies. Before vacation, the teachers collected their students' journals and set aside time to review and discuss them.

January

The buddy sessions resumed with a different focus. Because the Grade Ones had made noticeable improvements in their reading and writing, their teacher wanted to expand their audience for their personal writing. Now the Grade Sixes listened to them read not only picture books, but also their own stories and journal entries. In addition to the regular reading sessions, the buddies had a chance to go ice skating together. The Grade Sixes were a tremendous help in tying their buddies' skate laces, while the little ones were impressed with the skating styles of their buddies. With the second term well under way, another update letter, which included photocopies of pictures taken at the holiday party, was sent home.

February

With the buddy program routines well-established and the students feeling comfortable, response journal comments were positive, on the whole. Some students were even starting to plan for their buddy sessions and scrambling to complete friendship bracelets for their buddies. One problem that had surfaced was resolved by having the students concerned switch partners and then check in with the teacher on a weekly basis to let him know how they were doing. Overall, students were gaining confidence as readers, writers, and listeners.

March

Since January, the Grade Six students had been learning the rudiments of HyperCard, and they were now ready to apply their skills to a short-term technology project. The challenge was to create a HyperCard stack based on one of their buddies' stories. During the buddy sessions, the students collaborated to block the story and plan the illustrations. Then the Grade Sixes worked alone during computer time to create the HyperCard stacks.

April

After they completed their technology project, the Grade Sixes explained the steps and showed the finished products to their buddies. The Grade Ones became more aware of another computer application; at the same time, they were proud to see their stories presented in this new and different way. Once again, the teachers got together to look over the response journals as part of their ongoing monitoring of the buddy program.

May

The buddies were reading and writing about spring, and the Grade Ones were doing a unit entitled **Growing Things**. The Grade Six teacher had previously made arrangements with the principal and the caretaker to allow the reading buddies to do some gardening as a program extension. On a sunny day during one of their sessions, the children planted pansies in front of the school.

June

The buddy program was winding down, and several of the sessions had to be cancelled because of other school activities. In previous years, the Grade One teacher had included student comments about the program in his final parent letter. This year, however, he decided to try something new by having the Grade Sixes write to the families of their Grade One buddies. Among other things, they identified what they liked and disliked about the buddy program, which provided valuable information to the teachers and families alike. Besides offering another occasion to practise their letter writing skills, these letters heightened the Grade Sixes' awareness of their accomplishments.

The buddies also wrote farewell letters to each other. All of the letters, along with family comments and teacher observations, became the basis for evaluation and modifications for the following year.

A Note on Evaluation

In the course of a regular school day there are times when learning occurs in unplanned and unexpected situations. These teachable moments happen in buddy programs, as well. They become apparent as teachers listen to conversations between buddies and observe their interactions and reactions. In planning learning experiences, teachers can make use of

> Dear Sam
> Thak you for
> Being a woedrful
> reading Bue I
> enjuoda it very
> much I miss
> You a lot Plese
> right back
> from Lucas

the common interests of buddies, to the benefit of all. By making time available and involving both classes, teachers can alter the planned focus of future experiences to allow new and unexpected learning to occur.

Many teachers consider a reading buddy program to be an invaluable part of their curriculum and highly recommend it to others. Two such individuals, Dorena, who teaches Grade Five, and Bernadette, a Grade One teacher, implemented a book buddy program and found that students and their families were supportive beyond their expectations.

Reading stories to children strengthens the processes required for all learning. Reading is a source of personal enrichment and pleasure, and nowhere is this better experienced than in shared reading. In our small school, Grade One and Grade Five are situated across the hall from each other. This makes it very convenient for our two classes to incorporate a book buddy program into our language arts program. We meet twice in our six-day cycle.

Initially we explain to the older students how they can be reading models. We remind them to sit so that younger children can clearly see the print, to read with expression, and to encourage the younger child to join in, make predictions, raise questions, and discuss the illustrations. The Grade Five students gradually become aware that young children enjoy repetition and particularly like hearing the same story several times.

Grade One students are encouraged to choose their own books and, very often, the Grade Five students will bring along a book of special interest.

These emergent readers are exposed to and absorb many skills which aid them in becoming fluent. They learn the conventions of print, including directionality (left to right, top to bottom), become aware that print and pictures serve different functions, and soon begin to distinguish spacing and punctuation.

In addition to supporting emergent readers, our book buddy program nurtures healthy social interaction. The Grade Five students take on and enjoy new responsibilities: reading, helping to choose books, recording what has been read, giving stickers and other rewards, sharing on special occasions, helping the Grade Ones get dressed, working out playground difficulties, reporting to us on reading progress, and integrating our suggestions into their program.

For us, this experience is extremely rewarding. It is exciting to observe the contentment on the faces of these children and to see the Grade Five students becoming sensitive "care givers." As teachers, the knowledge that our students are sharing and learning together in a meaningful way is very rewarding.

Teacher Journal Entry

June 26

Well, my little ones have gone. I always feel so ambivalent about the end of the school year. Glad, but sad to see them go. I really need the time off to charge the ol' batteries and think about next year's crop, but then I feel terrible that I won't be working with the ones I've nurtured for the past 10 months.

June 27

While I was packing up, Edward came in. He's all excited about next year. He was talking to Allana, the Grade Seven teacher, and she was filling him in on some of his next year's students. Told him that the class is dynamite and that he's in for a great year. Guess what? He wants to share his good luck with me. He has some ideas for improving upon what we did this year and feels we can make some innovations, like having his students help mine on their neighborhood walk in the fall.

He remembered my griping about trying to find escorts for my 23 little ones to take them around the neighborhood. He could have his kids scout the neighborhood first and then develop a "treasure hunt" to provide a focus for the walk. Pretty soon he had me all fired up and I found myself brainstorming some ideas with him for next year. Wow, teaming with him was a super idea.

2 / Community Partners

June 23

How depressing. All the work this past year and I feel like I haven't accomplished anything. Why is that? I guess it was Jordan's comment that ticked me off. "Borrrrr—ing!" My first instincts were to blame him. I know he was being a smart aleck — but maybe he's right. Maybe I have done the same things the same way for too long. What can I do to make activities more relevant and exciting?

July 15

A few weeks off sure has improved my outlook. Am feeling much more positive, especially after thinking more about the idea that Angela sparked. "If that's what you want to happen, why don't you team your class with that community centre?" she asked. It sounded too ridiculous at first, but the more I thought about it, the more it started to make sense. It always takes one of those "ahaaas" to get the creative juices flowing. Yeah, why don't I? But where do I start?

August 21

Wow, where did the summer go? All of a sudden here I am, starting to gear up for school again. My phone call to the co-ordinator at the community centre was finally returned, and I've made an appointment to see her on Friday. Have to dig out the list of questions I prepared when I first had this bright idea. Also have to get over to school to sort through resources, organize lesson plans for the year, and see what's happening. That old beginning-of-school-year adrenalin rush returns.

August 30

Things are beginning to take shape. The co-ordinator was quite helpful and has a list of volunteers who could be paired with my students. She feels that

Patterns is an interesting theme and even made some suggestions on how it might work with her program — one group does quilting, another woodworking, and another astronomy. All of these activities involve patterns of a sort. Now all I have to do is present this plan to my students as a problem to be solved!

Community Partnerships

Community partnership programs connect students in a classroom with other people in their local community. Partnerships can be established with institutions or organizations such as seniors' residences or environmental groups, or simply with older or younger students in other schools. Activities within community partnerships can take many different forms, from writing to a pen pal in a nursing home to picking up litter in a community park.

By their nature, community partnership programs offer benefits to all concerned because they expand the experiences of both partners in a positive way and can increase self-esteem. The people whom students meet on a daily basis are generally close to their own ages and from similar backgrounds. At the same time, members of community institutions or organizations tend to relate to those with whom they have a great deal in common.

Partnerships provide authentic learning opportunities for cognitive and affective development. Links can be made across the curriculum, especially in language arts and social studies. Adult-student interaction encourages children to explore their role as citizens in ways that are meaningful to them right now and that will have relevance in the future. Children develop their social skills, become more aware of those around them, and broaden their sense of responsibility. Their enhanced awareness can lead to greater acceptance of others.

First-hand experience with the social, cultural, political, or business components of their community enables students to relate their classroom learning to the real world. More in-depth than field trips, community partnership programs put students in authentic settings which cannot be replicated in the classroom. Once there, students have the opportunity to learn from adults other than their teachers. The expertise, resources, and facilities available in community institutions provide effective, ready-made learning environments for students.

To people in the community, partnerships offer the opportunity to witness the acquisition and application of knowledge and skills through their interaction. This rewarding involvement allows them to gain a fresh perspective on life or tasks at hand. It generates feelings of satisfaction at having contributed to the growth of a young person and being appreciated for their efforts.

For all participants, partnerships provide opportunities for positive interactions with a wide range of people and contribute to breaking down negative stereotypes. It is for all these reasons that it is vital to increase opportunities for interaction by implementing community partnership programs.

Reaching Out

Teachers are generally aware of the many institutions or organizations found in the communities surrounding their schools, including seniors' residences, community centres, hospitals, churches, cultural associations, offices of special interest groups, high schools, colleges, and universities. They pass them on their way to school or have friends who have some connection to them. Once in a while their attention is drawn to special events sponsored by these potential community partners. Sometimes they hear comments or suggestions that trigger an insight, change their view of the organization, and prompt them to look for the interests that they have in common. If a partnership seems possible, then they are motivated to undertake a more thorough investigation which may require both persistence and patience. Teachers also may know of friends and relatives who can help recruit likely partners.

These preliminary investigations are useful groundwork for establishing contacts in the community, because building a community relationship is less straightforward than approaching teachers and classes in other schools. Who to approach in these groups depends upon the institutions and organizations concerned, but possible contacts might be program and activities co-ordinators, public relations staff, executive directors, administrators, presidents, chairpersons, subject consultants, department heads, or professors.

Background research will also often reveal the common ground between the school and the potential partner. Even though most institutions or organizations welcome educational contacts, this is not the main focus of their responsibilities, and they do not have a track record of working with students. Consequently, they may initially see only that they do not have the personnel, procedures, or programs in place to allow them to respond to educators' requests. Researching before contacting these organizations will allow teachers to address the reciprocal benefits to all concerned, the form a program might take, and how the program might run. Teachers can then work with community-based staff or volunteers to create and maintain partnerships that will meet the needs of the students and the members of the institutions or organizations alike.

Organizational Planning

Once an institution has been selected and its contact person has been reached, each group needs to become familiar with the other in preparation for working through the following details:

- program focus
- program duration
- frequency of sessions
- types of partner interaction
- preparing partners for the program
- involving families

Determining Program Focus

The form that the program takes will depend upon the nature of the participating organizations and their aims. Initial discussions may centre around issues such as the following: the proximity of the school to the community location, the age and health of the participants, the facilities at both locations, and possible groupings or pairings. Successful community programs engage partners in specific tasks that encourage positive interactions. With so many variables to consider, organizing a community partnership program requires open-mindedness, flexible thinking, and collaboration.

Determining Program Duration and Frequency

How long the partnership program will last and how many times the partners will interact should be decided in advance and tailored by the organizers to the aims of the program. Generally, community partner programs are long-term with regular, if not frequent, sessions. Continuity is an important factor in establishing and building the rapport necessary for success. With long-term programs, the school year affords sufficient time to incorporate seasonal and holiday activities.

At the same time, a long-term program does not necessarily mean organizing weekly carpools to a local institution. The program may include as few as three meetings a year or as many as two a month. Between meetings, students have time to follow up on the last one and prepare for the next. They may also maintain a correspondence with their partners between sessions. Regardless of the program's format, the blank **Time Line Planners** found on pages 16, 17, and 18 are a useful planning and tracking tool for partner sessions and other pertinent details.

Deciding on the Types of Partner Interaction

The types of partner interactions that will occur in the program are determined, once again, by how the teacher and the partner contact person define their respective programs. Community partners spend their time in a range of activities that may be either structured or spontaneous. They may meet to accomplish prepared tasks, such as participating in an organized tree-planting event. However, serendipitous experiences — for example, discovering a common interest in trains which leads to a joint trip to a train museum — are also valuable and should be identified and encouraged.

The backgrounds of the participants can be surveyed ahead of time so that their interests and personalities can be taken into account when matching partners or forming small groups. Participants might work together, take turns, or exchange roles — or not meet at all, as would occur in a community letter-writing project. Whether or not the partners meet face-to-face, both members of the partnership will get to know each other a little better, and enjoy doing so.

Preparing Partners for the Program

In the initial planning, teachers and their community contacts can exchange background information about their respective groups. At that time, teachers can make specific suggestions that will help the partners relate to young schoolchildren.

Since students will generally be partnered with adults, young adults, or teenagers, preparing them for their involvement in the program helps them develop positive and confident attitudes about their role in the partnership. Providing background information to them will increase their awareness of their partners. It will help them question stereotypes, respond appropriately to special needs, and behave accordingly. Being prepared is a necessary first step for demonstrating their competencies.

As community partners, students rely on their communication and social skills to get to know other people. This involves respect, listening, and sharing. A key aspect of preparation involves reviewing behavior guidelines, such as those found on page 27. Other preparation for the community partner program can take many forms:

- role-playing
- discussions
- brainstorming
- reading fiction
- viewing videos

Ideas and information can be exchanged by talking face-to-face, using audiotapes or videotapes, or writing from a distance. Preparation at the appropriate level benefits students and contributes to the overall success of the program.

Involving Families

As in any other program, families welcome information regarding their children's activities and personal comments about their progress. At the outset, the community partner program can be outlined in a letter to the family, with update letters sent home at appropriate intervals to keep everyone apprised as the program unfolds. Newsletters are also useful for informing families about program milestones and progress. In addition to lending general support, families often willingly volunteer to assist with program activities. Teachers always appreciate when others can help to handle arrangements, contact the local media, or accompany the class to partner sessions. Families share in the feelings of success and satisfaction felt by all participants when they receive final update letters and are included in end-of-year celebrations.

Curriculum Planning

As the organizational planning goes forward, teachers can explore the possible meeting points in the curriculum for the program as they consider the following:

- subject area or theme focus
- curriculum integration
- specific projects
- program extensions
- program assessment

Subject Area or Theme Focus

Community partner programs tend to have strong linkages to social studies and language arts. Students learn about themselves and their community and at the same develop their communication skills. In addition, however, specific projects carried out within a program can have a particular subject area focus; in fact, there are imaginative ways to include most subject areas in community partner programs, especially when children can draw upon the backgrounds and interests of the partners.

Curriculum Integration

Integration takes place in the classroom and during partner sessions and forges links among main subject areas as well as incidental ones.

For example, a theme with **Changes** as its focus can integrate language arts, social studies, health, social skills, research skills, and technology. In their theme study, students may be challenged to learn how the community has evolved and changed by exploring local history and geography. As one part of their research, they gather first-hand accounts of changes from elderly partners who are members of the local community centre. As they research, students discover that tape recorders are very handy when they are gathering information from primary sources, but they must negotiate the use of such devices with their partners. During the course of their conversations and interviews, students become aware of the ageing process, prompting them to discuss age and youth in health class. When their research focus shifts to secondary sources, students may teach their partners how to access computerized information at the local library. In this way, many areas of the curriculum are integrated.

Specific Projects

When the overall program is in place and time is allotted, partners can devote themselves to particular short-term activities to add variety, reinforce special interests, and sustain their motivation. In the case of one community partnership program, students who were studying environmental science were paired with members of a local action group whose overall aim was to promote the revitalization of a river valley. Partners participated in regularly scheduled outdoor activities — hiking in the valley, identifying plants and wildlife, and monitoring pollution. As a special project during the winter months, the partners spent a few weeks working in small groups to construct bird houses which they placed throughout the valley in the spring. In the ongoing activities, students developed their science knowledge and their communication skills; the special project introduced them to different building materials and simple woodworking skills.

Program Extensions

Extensions, as with short-term projects, are a way to interject a change of pace into community partner programs. Ideas for them can come from either side of the partnership. Partner groups have special interests and celebrations to share with students. Students have many talents and can contribute music and drama presentations. Either group can initiate seasonal, holiday, and birthday parties, as well as introductory and culminating events for the program. Partners might enjoy going on field trips or attending special functions together. Whatever the extension or special short-term project, it is well worth taking a few pictures and writing a brief article to share the event with the school, organization, and community at large.

Response journals complement community partner programs, and students benefit from keeping them. Because partner programs are activity-based and characterized by personal interactions in different settings, they provide stimulation and motivate students to become actively involved. Taking part in program activities which, for them, are out of the ordinary generates thoughts and ideas as well as the desire to express them. Students should be encouraged to reflect upon their experiences, using separate notebooks to capture their personal responses. These journals become records of personal, social, and academic development over the course of the program.

Response journals are one of the many evaluation tools that teachers can use to assess their students' progress. Along with the usual assessment of academic knowledge and skills, partner interactions are observed and monitored throughout the program. With guidance, students demonstrate their competencies and fine-tune the appropriate behaviors and attitudes on which they focussed as they prepared for the program. The community partners can become involved as well by completing questionnaires in which they provide feedback about the students and the program itself.

Student participation in community partnership programs provides opportunities for them to demonstrate their task commitment and time management skills. Their sense of ownership and feelings of responsibility can also be observed, both directly and through conversations with their older partners.

A Sample Time Line — A Year at a Glance

Because of the broad range of activities and resources available in any community, no one time line can be representative of how a community partnership program might look and how it will evolve over the course of the year. The time line in this chapter outlines how one such program worked with students in Grades Two and Five and residents of a retirement community. The program used shared reading to expand an ongoing reading buddies program established in the school. Implementation necessitated local fund raising and included a special pro-

Sample Community Partner Timeline

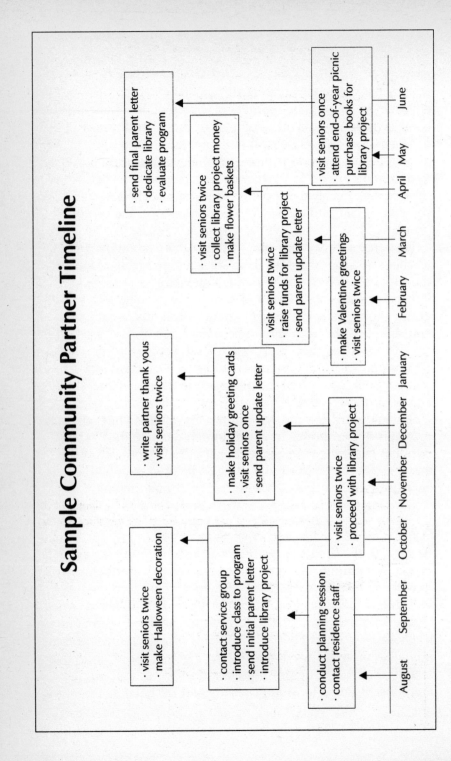

Timeline months: August · September · October · November · December · January · February · March · April · May · June

- visit seniors twice
- make Halloween decoration

- contact service group
- introduce class to program
- send initial parent letter
- introduce library project

- conduct planning session
- contact residence staff

- write partner thank yous
- visit seniors twice

- make holiday greeting cards
- visit seniors once
- send parent update letter

- visit seniors twice
- proceed with library project

- visit seniors twice
- raise funds for library project
- send parent update letter

- make Valentine greetings
- visit seniors twice

- visit seniors twice
- collect library project money
- make flower baskets

- send final parent letter
- dedicate library
- evaluate program

- visit seniors once
- attend end-of-year picnic
- purchase books for library project

Coventry Village Grant Application

Goals
The following statements are the goals for the program:
- develop a purpose (reason) for reading
- enhance intergenerational relationships
- foster respect for the elderly
- strengthen relationships among students, parents, teachers, and the community
- continue and expand a pilot program begun last year

Community
Parents of students will accompany classes to Coventry Retirement Living Community. The Marketing Manager and Program Director from Coventry will provide an orientation for students and parents to their retirement village. Residents of the village will participate in a reading experience with children.

Program
Fifty elementary students in Grades Two and Five will read with at least 20 Coventry residents twice a month. Partnerships will be developed with one second grader, one fifth grader, and a Coventry resident. They will share books with each other for 20 minutes. Coventry will conduct an orientation for the students before their first visit to the village. On special occasions, the students will create small gifts for their village partner. A videotape and 35mm photos of the year's activities will be produced during the year. The year will culminate with a picnic at Coventry.

Evaluation
Enthusiasm will be reflected in the 35mm photos and videotape. A written survey will be developed and administered to the students on their reactions and feelings about the experience.

Budget

Supplies	canvas tote bags
	arts and crafts supplies for small gifts
	film and videotape
	year-end picnic supplies
Travel	weekly shuttle bus
	bus for the year-end picnic

ject to create a mini-library of children's literature at the retirement community.

August

Before the new school year started, the Grade Two and Grade Five teachers met to plan for the year and complete a grant proposal to the school foundation for funding, as shown on page 51. Contact with the retirement community was made to discuss plans. It was discovered that as a result of staffing changes over the summer, the retirement community had a new marketing director, but the same program director would be part of their team. It was necessary to bring the new director up to date on the program, and so she was invited to visit the school.

September

The teachers wrote to a local service group outlining the special project and requested funds.

With that under way, students and their families were introduced to the program. An initial parent letter was sent home.

September 10

Dear Parents,

We are ready to begin a Community Partners Program, an intergenerational program connecting our children with seniors in a local residence. My Grade Two class, along with Mrs L.'s Grade Fives, will visit the residents of Coventry Village to share books each month throughout the school year. Your child will have a Grade Five partner as well as a Coventry partner.

The program director will be here in our room next Wednesday at 2:00 p.m. to discuss the program. You are welcome to visit and learn more about our plans.

Looking forward to seeing you then and having your ongoing support in this new program.

Mrs K.

An orientation was conducted which included a visit from the residents of the retirement community. Discussion and questions helped to make participants feel comfortable about one another. Teachers wrote a letter to the marketing director and the program director requesting the retirement community's support for the special library project.

October

Seniors were matched with students so that each senior had a Grade Two and a Grade Five partner. A timetable was set up with alternating grade visits to the seniors. The students selected Halloween books from the school library for their first visits. They also brought copies of the school newsletter and their hand-made Halloween decorations.

November

The students continued their visits, bringing favorite books from home to share with their partners. The marketing director informed the teachers that the retirement community had agreed to participate in the library project. The community would match the funds raised by the students — equivalent to the purchase of a book a month.

December

This month, the students prepared an entertainment program for their joint holiday visit by practising festive songs and creating cards for their partners. In turn, the seniors presented their student partners with hand-made book marks. The principal attended the celebration. A parent update letter was sent home to review the fall term's activities and look ahead to the winter term.

January

As part of their language arts curriculum, both classes wrote and mailed thank-you letters to their partners — and were delighted to receive a thank-you note in return.

Because of inclement weather, one of the visits had to be rescheduled. This month the books for shared reading were supplied by the seniors.

February

Students designed Valentine greetings to take along on their regular visits. Books on a Valentine theme suggested by the teacher librarian were taken for their readings.

March

The students visits continued. The teachers were pleased to receive notification that the service club would support their library project by purchasing a book a month. A parent update letter was sent home to share the good news and to explain how families could help their children raise funds by doing chores around the house.

April

As the children earned their chore money, it was accumulated in the book fund. In anticipation of their May visit, the students created paper flower baskets for their partners. They made their usual reading visits. Some children elected to bring books about their traditional spring holidays.

May

The students visited their partners at the beginning of the month, taking along books from the public library and their May flower baskets. To prepare for an end-of-the-year family picnic later in the month at the retirement community, the teachers sent home an invitation well in advance.

Everyone who attended the picnic enjoyed the puppet shows, May Pole dancing, and a slide presentation, along with good food and great company. All the funds raised for the library project were now used to purchase a selection of hardcover books.

June

A final parent letter inviting them to the library dedication ceremony at the retirement community was sent home. Because this was the students' last visit, they presented the new books and their school yearbook as part of the ceremony. Light refreshments were served and the partners said good-bye to one another. The teachers, marketing director, and program director met at the end of the month to share feedback from the residents and the students as part of their evaluation of the program.

Community Partnership Success Stories

Community partnership programs are not a new phenomenon; in fact, they have been quietly happening for some time. Teachers, always ready to involve students in meaningful activities, have diligently looked to their communities to support their educational objectives. What has changed, on the part of more and more teachers, is the degree of interest in reaching out into the community. With fewer dollars to go around and the cry for a more relevant curriculum that will carry today's students into the future, teachers have had to become even more creative in finding educational environments beyond the classroom. The following are three success stories from educators whose partnership programs broadened the skills and knowledge of their students while at the same time enriching their communities.

Lincoln School - Coventry Village Seniors Partners in Reading
by Lorna Engwall

In the summer a few years ago, I met with the Lincoln School Improvement Team to review our local assessment results and make plans for the coming year. Our major area of focus for improvement was in reading. As we discussed the impact of a variety of instructional methodologies and materials, we also brainstormed ways to involve parents and the community in promoting reading with our students. It was from these discussions that the idea of a reading partnership with a local nursing home was born.

Jeanne Kuba, a Grade Two teacher, and Lisa Lobdell, who teaches Grade Five, had already developed a "partners in reading" program with their students in the school, and so they decided to take this partnership to the community. They chose Coventry Village because Jeanne had a close friend who was a resident there, and, as a result, she knew that the idea would be well-received by the staff and residents.

Jeanne and Lisa established a working relationship with the activities director at Coventry and soon designed a program to pair one Coventry resident with one second-grader and one fifth-grader for the school year. The students bring books to Coventry on alternating weeks and read them with their partners. Some of the residents are able to read books to the students as well; however, most enjoy listening to the children reading to them. Holidays are always marked with special celebrations. Initially, it was the Lincoln students who made gifts and entertained the residents; however, in the past two years we have seen an increase in the level of involvement from Coventry, and the residents are proud to present hand-made gifts to the children on special occasions, as well. An end-of-the-year picnic has become a tradition enjoyed by the residents, students, Coventry staff, teachers, and many parents.

Each fall, members of the Coventry staff and a few residents visit Lincoln School to discuss the program with our students. They help to prepare the students for this unique experience and try to alleviate any fears they may have. A slide program which helps to show the students what they will experience has been created through the efforts of the Coventry staff and the Lincoln teachers.

During the last school year, the teachers, joined by our Chapter 1 reading teacher, decided to develop a children's library at Coventry for the use of the children who visit relatives or friends there. To purchase the books for the library, students were asked to do small chores around the home to raise money, which was then matched by our local Kiwanis Club.

Coventry purchased a new bookcase to hold the books and also contributed toward the cost of the books. A special dedication ceremony and celebration was held at the end of the year when our students presented the books to the centre. Each year, our students will continue to add to this very special library!

Last fall, we were able to expand the program to include two more classes, another Grade Two and another Grade Five. Half of the Grade Twos and half of the Grade Fives visit each week while the remaining students work with their reading partners at school, allowing us to send a group of about 25 students to Coventry every week. In this way, the residents of Coventry are assured of a visitor every week during the entire school year. Since many of them seldom have visitors, they look forward to seeing their special partners each week.

The benefits of this kind of partnership are numerous. Though originally designed to promote reading by our students, it has also taught everyone the value of intergenerational relationships.

Many children (and adults) lack exposure to the elderly and are uncomfortable around them because they do not know how to relate to them. Nursing homes, like hospitals, can be very frightening places for children to visit. Going to Coventry with their teacher and other students lessens the fear and allows the students the opportunity to form real friendships with their resident partner by reading and talking to them. Many parents have also become involved in the program and visit regularly. Some have encouraged their child to visit their resident partner outside of school and continue the relationship after the child has moved to another grade.

Yes, we have had to deal with the illness and death of residents. However, this also provides an opportunity to help children deal with their fears. Experiencing the death of a resident and discussing their feelings with their teacher and classmates can help children deal with personal losses in their own families. Our school librarian has purchased numerous books which deal with this topic in a healthy manner and are suitable for teachers to use with their classes.

Our only problem in continuing this program each year has been the constant changes in staff at Coventry. As with most facilities for the elderly, it is difficult to keep employees for a long term. Our teachers have developed very good working relationships with the activities directors, only to see them leave during the year, which means we then have to begin again with a new person. We are beginning our fifth year, though, and so it is obvious that both facilities are benefiting from this very special partnership and are committed to continuing it!

Haliburton Highlands Project E.L.M.

David Mowat, who teaches senior biology at Haliburton Highlands Secondary School, got started with Project E.L.M. (Energy, Lifestyles, Materials) when two ideas coalesced, and a really keen Grade Three-Four teacher gave him the impetus. He and the other teacher were both members of their school board's environmental action committee and were helping to develop Earth Day activities.

At the same time, Dave had to develop a viable environmental project for his biology class, and he had chosen a business model to carry out his plans. For the business model, his students needed to serve clients and fill a demand in the market. Having been previously involved in YMCA camps, Dave placed a high value on doing service in the community. He saw the benefits of establishing positive contact and developing trust between young children and teenagers and looked to helping to nurture young children in the community. The students of the Grade Three-Four teacher became the first clients of his own students.

Dave and his students developed a business plan and prepared a brochure to present to the school board. The completed plan entailed creating a concept path, a trail on unused acreage behind the high school, for an Earth Week program to take place in the spring.

In developing the program, Dave drew in other subjects, pulled in all the elements of the current Ministry of Education curriculum, and involved his students in lateral thinking. The class designed original activities and involved students in English, drama, and art, as well as in biology. At the conclusion of the first year, they found that the program was successful beyond their expectations and that they had created a new service for future classes.

In the next year, Dave's class worked with three other classes: a Grade One-Two, a Grade Four, and a Grade Five. In the fall his students visited the elementary school to interact with their clients. They introduced themselves and the service they had to offer, and they supplied classroom teachers with letters and brochures to use in their home-school communications.

Class time during the year was used to design the activities for E.L.M. Dave selected student volunteers to be trail leaders who would train in leadership and conceptualize the trail. Another group of student volunteers teamed up with a community organization, Friendship Earth, to build the trail. Members of Friendship Earth taught students about the woods, marked out the trail, cleared it, and built bridges. Drama students rehearsed their roles for the trail. Art students made drawings, designs, trail plans, and signs. All of the students were involved in creating stories and scripts for stations on the trail. Two weeks before the event, the senior students returned to the elementary school class to play games and prepare the younger children for the trail.

On the specified day, the children spent the morning and afternoon on the trail, breaking only for lunch. They hiked and participated in activities at stations along the trail in small groups led by one of the trained high school students. Activities were designed to have a concrete component. Artifacts made by the art students were eagerly collected by the young children. They had brought along their hand-made souvenir bags for the occasion. One of the trail activities included a puppet show with tree characters that helped the youngest students identify trees by the bark.

The young children responded to their environmental experience through class discussion, drawing, and writing about it. The Grade Four class even conducted an experiment based on what they had learned.

Project E.L.M. provided many opportunities for learning. The educational setting provided the high school students with a real-life experience. In implementing a business project, they developed and used skills they could transfer to other real-life situations. They learned to tailor each year's program to the ever-changing needs of client classes. Younger students benefited as well. Through their participation in this program, they experienced care, attention, and positive teenage role models.

Archie Stouffer - Hyland Crest Pen Pal Partners
by Bonnie Berry

During the past seven years, I have used a pen pal program between my Grade Five students and residents of Hyland Crest Senior Citizens' Home as a major component of my language arts program.

Hyland Crest is situated within easy walking distance of our school. This has made it convenient for delivering the mail pouch and visiting our pen pals.

The program was initially suggested to me by my grandmother who is a resident at Hyland Crest. With the assistance of the activities director, we were able to develop a plan which has evolved over the years into an enjoyable and valuable project between my students and the seniors.

Each year, the activities director provides me with a list of residents who are willing and able to participate in the letter writing. I have come to know many of the residents and am able to pair them effectively with my students. To assist the residents who are unable to do the actual writing of the letters, we have a volunteer at Hyland Crest, called the ghost writer, who helps some of the residents. Some, like my grandmother, require assistance because of poor eyesight. Some are unable to hold a pen because of arthritis or other physical disabilities. The ghost writer's assistance has been invaluable.

The initial stages of the program consist of the students writing autobiographical material as introductions to their pen pals. The seniors responded in a similar fashion.

After they exchange two or three letters, I arrange a visit to Hyland Crest. At that time, the students meet their pen pals, have a tour of the facility, and share refreshments and conversation with the residents. I feel that this initial visit serves the purpose of helping the students better to understand and appreciate the environment in which the residents live. It also fosters an awareness of the characteristics of the audience for whom the children are writing. After our first visit, we are able to discuss the special needs of our pen pals and to develop an awareness of the writing style appropriate in our letters.

Every event that happens in our school or home life provides material for our letters. We have a posted list of pen pal topics that is constantly updated by anyone with ideas for our letters. When the mail pouch arrives, letters are distributed, shared, and then taken home to read to parents. I have found that families are very positive and supportive of this program. They encourage their children to write extra letters from home and sometimes take them to Hyland Crest for weekend visits.

The students are encouraged to send copies of their creative writing and art to their pen pals. In December, we make wreaths as a craft project and give them to the pen pals as a special gift. Birthdays are remembered with cards and sometimes with small gifts.

As a special conclusion to the program, we are invited to Hyland Crest in June each year for a barbecue lunch. After the lunch, the students present a program of talent for the residents to enjoy. Usually at this time, all the residents at Hyland Crest,

Coventry Village Retirement Home

When I go to Coventry Village it makes me feel like I'm making the residents happy. It's fun fun entertaining them. I'm glad that I can help and they know that they have someone who cares about them. I like being useful to them because when I was younger and my mom read to me, it made me feel important. Now I'm reading to them and I hope they feel important when I'm reading. I love reading to them because it makes me the one they're listening to. Their family has gone and grown up so we have to make them feel like we're their daughter or son. We make them feel welcome so when I see them smiling I know they enjoy our reading.

My resident just enjoys seeing me. She compliments me.

not just the pen pals, join us. It is a happy, exciting time for everyone.

The rewards of this program are tremendous. The children develop an understanding and appreciation of the ageing process. They also show a sensitivity to the special needs of the residents who have disabilities. They learn to share information with their pen pals about topics we are studying in class. A popular unit is our **Pioneer Unit**, which provides many topics for back and forth sharing of information. We visit Black Creek Pioneer Village each year, and the students are enthusiastic as they share this experience.

Evaluation is done through process writing conferencing and ongoing feedback throughout the program, some of it from their journals.

Our evaluation scale for parent reporting is a two-fold system of achievement and effort. Achievement ratings are assigned for all subject areas, and effort is rated as Outstanding, Good, Satisfactory, or Insufficient. I use these ratings for each letter.

This program generates a great deal of enthusiasm in my class, but there are challenges to take into account. There are not always enough seniors to write all the letters. My class size has grown and the number of residents has not always grown accordingly. However, with some seniors taking two pen pals and even more help from our ghost writer, we have been able to overcome this.

Two of the seniors have died during the program. We always discuss this possibility in the first few weeks and attempt to be prepared. Although stressful for us to deal with, the death of a pen pal was a learning experience when it happened. Families do not tend to live near grandparents as much now as in previous generations, and for many children, these pen pals become surrogate grandparents, with all the blessings and benefits that entails.

Teacher Journal Entry

December 21

Mr. Morgan has died! How on earth can I face the children with this news? More importantly, what can I tell Jake? Mr. Morgan was the grandparent he never knew. After seeing Jake come out of his shell with this friendship, I dread breaking the news. No, I have to focus on the positive. They looked so happy just the other day at our holiday celebration. Their bird house project was finished and Jake was so proud of his reading to Mr. Morgan. I prepared the children for the possibility of one of the residents dying, but the reality is now here and I have to deal with it when we come back in January.

January 5

The day I dreaded came, and you know what? I discovered two valuable insights into my children. In spite of my fears, Jake has a quiet strength that I've never seen. And for all their sometimes-teasing behaviors, my children can respond sensitively to a crisis. When Jake broke down and cried, the kids were super. They accepted his sorrow and tried cheering him up. Sarah reminded Jake of how Mr. Morgan remembered all their names. Even Nikolai put in a good word about all the nice visits with Mr. Morgan.

January 6

Today, Jake, with the help of Raven, Ahmad, and Kirby, put together a touching memorial service to honor Mr. Morgan — veteran of World War II, former owner of the local corner store, husband, and father to Bill, Jennifer, and Janine. The children must have been listening to his stories and recollections even more closely than I had thought.

3 / Pen Pals and Cyberpals

December 8

Finally managed to get our holiday information package out. My students put their little hearts into getting the last-minute things done. Corina's class should get the package in about a week (cross my fingers). I hope I gave it enough time. Sending things out by snail mail does have its advantages, though. The greeting cards and hand-made decorations were so creative — Jerald certainly has a flair for using sparkles. I think Corina's class will enjoy them. It'll be even better when she gets her computers set up with the modem so we can send our letters by e-mail. First, she said they would have them by October, then it was November, and now she says January. Who knows?

January 9

Hey, what a pleasant surprise — I got an e-mail message from Corina! She is on-line, finally. They received the package on their last day of school. I can't believe my good luck. I was really worried when I got their information package in good time, and ours went out later. So much to catch up on. Wait until my kids log in next week and get their first e-mail letters. Corina said she's planning to have her group send their thanks via the computer. Now if I can only contain myself and not let the cat out of the bag. It'll be hard for me knowing the excitement it'll cause.

January 17

Bedlam and delight! I told the kids we were going to use e-mail today, and they saw New Year's greetings waiting for them from you know who. Well, am I glad I had my camera. Capturing Saskia's toothy grin on film was worth my enforced silence. Even Alvin, who's never been known for his sociability, went gangbusters. He was telling anybody, whether they listened to him or not, what his pen pal had written (this from a student who hasn't shared much of his life with anyone). Now they can't wait to compose their responses and send them back.

Pen Pal Partnerships

Pen pal partnerships connect students in one school to students in another anywhere in the world.

Setting up and maintaining exchanges between pen pals, whether within the community, nationally, or internationally, has long been a popular school focus. Often, educators who meet at conferences or on other occasions discover they teach the same grade and share an interest in having an authentic motivation for their students to communicate in writing with others. Children benefit from relating to peers outside their immediate school environment. They discover the common strands in their own and their pen pals' lives — families, pets, favorites, birthdays, and holidays. Their increased awareness and new-found knowledge carries over into their daily lives. When students hear newscasts, current events, or sports, they often pay closer attention as a result of their involvement in a pen pal program.

Pen pal programs add a real-life component to the curriculum. They present opportunities for students to extend their comprehension. In the letter-writing process, thinking skills come to the fore. Students assume a responsive and empathic role by noting details, developing their questioning skills, and becoming critical thinkers. Evidence of this appears in the content of their communications and carries over into their daily lives.

With current technology, pen pal correspondence may be transformed from the traditional pen-and-paper approach to that of computer and modem. The same planning is required and the same results occur when cyberpals (sometimes also called *key pals* or *net pals*) correspond. Teachers who have operated successful pen pals projects can easily transfer their familiar activities to computers. They are also pleased by the quicker response times their students experience.

Writing to pen pals or e-mailing to cyberpals fits into all areas of the curriculum because students share experiences about life at home and school. Whether the class has gained a new member, attended Carnival, or visited a museum, students want to communicate this. When students share similar themes and topics, they have a common ground for writing.

Students can choose regular mail or e-mail if the technology is available. When the correspondence has a sense of urgency, e-mail offers an opportunity for immediate, abbreviated dialogue between two people, who still always have the option to expand on the e-mail message by writing an in-depth letter. Students may also write out their work on projects, upload or mail them with the research, and wait for a response. In these ways, their class activities become the focus for shared communication in a social context.

Reaching Out

The first step toward implementing a pen pal program is to make contact with another teacher. Any number of people can provide resources or contact points that will allow the distribution of a **Teacher Information Sheet**, as shown on page 14:

- consultants, who can provide names of like-minded teachers
- colleagues who have moved to new schools or cities
- participants in professional development sessions
- contacts made through teaching or other educational organizations or publications
- friends or relatives in other cities or countries
- acquaintances from annual class trips to other cities
- Internet contacts

Because they visit many schools and are familiar with the curriculum in a variety of classes, consultants are in an excellent position to refer the names of teachers with similar interests. Teachers who have moved on to other schools or school systems may be prepared to establish communication links with a class at their former school and in this way continue their friendships with students and teachers alike. As teachers become acquainted with other educators when they attend professional development courses, workshops, or conferences, they can make a point of sharing their interest in a pen pal arrangement.

If classes in a school already make an annual trip to another city, this could be an occasion for teachers to establish contacts leading to a pen pal program, which may eventually provide another authentic purpose for making the visit.

Additional opportunities present themselves in other ways. Many educational journals and publications mention authors and their affiliations at the end of their articles so that readers can contact them. Teacher magazines, such as *Learning: Successful Teaching Today*, often have sections like "Reader Exchange" devoted to teachers who are seeking pen pals for their classes. As well, magazines and newsletters devoted to educational use of the Internet, such as *Classroom Connect*, encourage cyberpals with services similar to its "Email Cyberpal Connection" service.

Friends and relatives, especially those with children of school age, are valuable resources who can provide introductions to educators in their school districts. In annual school trips, students may meet others with whom they would like to keep in touch by letter or e-mail. Once again, these trips also provide an opportunity for like-minded educators to share their views and to strike up friendships that may lead to pen pal programs.

Finally, an ever-growing resource is the Internet. More and more teachers are becoming familiar with the newest way to communicate globally using computers. They log on to bulletin boards, join conferences, and explore the World Wide Web as they surf the Internet. This modern resource opens up channels that no one would have believed possible a few years ago, and teachers can make contacts with other educators who are also interested in developing pen pal relationships. Regardless of the mode of contact, when two teachers have agreed to a pen pal relationship, their planning focusses on a number of factors.

Organizational Planning

After the contact has been made either by phone or by electronic or surface mail, discussion and planning for the school year will sort out the organizational details. Important details or issues to resolve include the following:

- program duration
- frequency of correspondence
- matching students
- the medium of correspondence
- content of information packages
- involving families

Determining Program Duration

There are advantages for students in sustaining a year-long pen pal relationship. This time span affords continuity for both parties, who start off as strangers and come to know each other better by sharing experiences in their lives. In a year-long program, there are more opportunities to develop projects related to the curriculum than there are in a shorter-term project. The seasons, holidays, and birthdays provide stimulation for discussion. The teacher also benefits from the cohesive, integrated program that results from intense, long-term planning. Once in place, such a plan is readily adapted for future use.

This is not to exclude correspondence over a shorter term, however. If the goals are specific or the time is limited, especially in the upper grades, then a correspondence of short duration is suitable. For example, two French classes in neighboring school systems might exchange a couple of letters in order to use their second language in a purposeful exercise. In such a program, there is still time to send a class photo album and to stage a culminating activity such as a group gathering. Students could enjoy a picnic at a location between the two schools, or actually participate in an exchange visit.

Determining the Frequency of Correspondence

Based on the grade and skill level of the students, the teachers determine how often correspondence is to be exchanged. At the lower grades, one letter per term allows time for the teaching and modelling of letter-writing skills and format. At the middle grades, monthly letter writing might be practised after an introductory unit. At the upper grades, a brief overview of letter writing might be followed by frequent, independent, personal correspondence.

Matching Students

Ideally, class sizes will be the same, but if one class is larger than the other, several of its students may be asked to have more than one pen pal. Students whose reading and writing skills allow them to work independently are good candidates for the extra task; however, there may be other factors to consider. Students who are challenged by regular reading and writing activities can be highly motivated when given the opportunity for authentic communication with someone they are getting to know better. The prospect of making new acquaintances is an incentive for these students to take on the responsibility of corresponding with more than one pen pal. The payoff is tangible — two letters when everyone else receives one.

Deciding on the Medium of Correspondence

Today, correspondence can travel either by regular mail or electronically. Traditionally, students have used pencil, pen, and paper to write their letters. Pictures were drawn in pencil crayon or painted. Their work was exchanged through the postal service, which is still a valuable means of communication because everyone has access to a post office. With more schools being equipped with computers, printers, and modems, however, technology can broaden the types of communications available, and interchanges are potentially quicker and more frequent. Students can choose to enter their text and design graphics on computer and then mail their printouts or e-mail their work directly over the Internet. Older students who work on computer can be shown how to make a reusable date and address template and save it as a current letter.

Deciding on the Content of Information Packages

The focus of the correspondence is usually to exchange letters, but other relevant items can be included in the information packages exchanged between the two classrooms. Whether handwritten or computer-generated, especially in the lower and middle grades, individual letters are placed together in a large envelope or small box for mailing. Whenever possible, items such as class or school newsletters, yearbooks, video and audio tapes, newspapers, postcards, pictures, posters, or maps can be added. Older students, who may be corresponding independently, may also be working on a class project which the teachers have planned. In such a case, students would be responsible for mailing their own letters, but the information package that the teacher sends would include their project work.

Involving Families

Depending on the nature of the classes and the age and maturity of the students, teachers need to find appropriate ways to inform families about ongoing correspondence. As with other class activities, it is important with a pen pal program to maintain a strong home-school connection. It is always appropriate to send introductory and final notes home to families. They can be informed by newsletters or bulletin board displays, or through information packages that are sent home to be shared.

For younger children, family update letters may be sent home to mark the sending and receiving of information packages as well as to advise of special events. If information packages are to include photographs or items belonging to a student, families should be notified so that they can help their children collect appropriate artifacts. Family members might be persuaded to assist with preparing the package or perhaps supporting the mailing costs. Individual letters become part of the students' homework that is taken home to be shared with their families. Families enjoy reading pen pal letters with their children, and they can encourage their children to write friendly, informative letters to their pen pals throughout the year. Older students may prefer to share informally with their families what they learn from and about their pen pals. At the end of the school year, some students may want to continue the correspondence with their pen pals. To facilitate this, teachers could send a letter home to obtain parental permission for sharing home addresses.

Curriculum Planning

As the planning discussions continue, additional curriculum details need to be sorted out as well. These include the following:

- subject area or theme focus
- curriculum integration
- specific joint pen pal projects
- exchange visits
- program extensions
- program assessment

Subject Area or Theme Focus

Generally, at the beginning of the fall term, teachers have an overview of the themes, topics, or units they are going to cover during the school year. They have investigated related materials in the library resource centre, and they know the learning outcomes they will assess. Sharing these ideas ahead of time with pen pal teachers allows both teachers to brainstorm and to contribute to the implementation of the program in a variety of ways. For example, if the other teacher's students will be studying urban environments, the home teacher and her class can gather material about their city. Then this primary research, which is often unique, can be included in their information package and mentioned in their letters.

Curriculum Integration

A pen pal program can easily be integrated into a range of subject areas across the curriculum. Whether the correspondence is written by hand or on the computer, it is an authentic language arts experience because it includes creative writing, reading, and listening. In putting their thoughts down, students are involved in a writing and editing process in which they address style, vocabulary, grammar, punctuation, and capitalization, as well as the conventions of letter writing. When letters and packages are delivered to the classroom, they are highlights which students capture in their journals and record on classroom calendars.

Students also enjoy sharing their letters and e-mail with classmates, reading buddies, and parents. The contents of the correspondence provide interesting social studies and science springboards. City students may write to their pen pals about using a subway, and island students may tell about taking a ferry. These informal sources of information about lifestyles and environments are enriching.

When students communicate by e-mail, there is a sense of immediacy and ownership because they are using current, state-of-the-art technology. Using e-mail for correspondence introduces students to telecommunications while, at the same time, integrating the pen pal program into the technology component of the curriculum. Students who gain experience with technology now are better prepared to become responsible, independent learners and make informed decisions about the increasing access to the Internet in the future.

Specific Joint Pen Pal Projects

As well as the regular exchange of letters which goes smoothly once it is started, especially with older students, the teachers concerned may have the time and energy to develop projects that are complementary and specific to the pen pals. For example, if both pen pals read and review a novel set in the locale of the other, there is an added dimension to the appreciation of the story. Living in different places, they bring differing points of view to tasks requiring comparison and contrast.

Another possible special project uses Sign Out Science bags. Students either write down or enter and save the contents and projects of their SOS bags, along with their results. All pertinent information is mailed or uploaded to their pen pals, who conduct the experiments and communicate their results for comparison. (For more information about these activities, see *Sign Out Science*, 1993.)

Some other joint project ideas to consider are the following:

- publish a joint newsletter
- write stories and exchange them for illustration
- collect and amalgamate family tree data

Exchange Visits

If the pen pals are within a reasonable travelling distance, an exchange visit adds immeasurably to the pen pal program and provides opportunities for a broad range of language and problem-solving activities. In preparation for an exchange visit, students create invitations and plan the visit. When the pen pals arrive, their partners greet them, they participate in an ice-breaking activity, and then they go on a tour of the school. Special activities, such as a walking tour of the main street, lunch together, or making a craft to take home, are planned. The pen pal visit could become an annual school trip.

Program Extensions

In addition to regular correspondence and special projects, other opportunities, which often do not involve extra planning or writing, may present themselves and allow teachers to extend pen pal programs. Many schools publish newsletters on a regular basis, and some classes produce their own newsletters. These are good informal sources of information about the school and can be included in information packages. Newsletters communicate a holistic picture of the school community as they focus on the kinds of clubs that are available, popular activities, and the people involved in them.

Another way to exchange incidental information is to take advantage of family travels to the pen pals' city. Family members could be asked to bring back postcards or newspapers, deliver the information packages, or even talk to the class about their pen pals' home town. Getting first-hand information from a personal source helps to broaden students' general knowledge and to enrich their dialogue.

Teachers can extend and share the excitement of receiving information packages by talking about them at assemblies and displaying the contents. The classroom is a good place to start, a hallway is better, but the best place of all is the foyer of the school. In the foyer, information packages can be viewed by more people, including visitors to the school who may be curious enough to talk to the children about the program. The resulting high profile broadens the exposure of the pen pal program, which in turn motivates those involved. Sending a photograph of the display and written comments about it to the originating class offers a way to share this motivation. Students see how seriously their efforts are taken and are encouraged to maintain high standards in their future correspondence.

Correspondence often creates friendships that go beyond the time frame of the classroom. As the end of the school year approaches, students naturally feel sad to end their association. Sharing their home addresses not only provides them with the choice to continue, but also allows them to lay the foundation for a long-term correspondence. After all, it is possible they may meet in the future, especially if they visit relatives in the vicinity of their pen pals.

Program Assessment

When starting out with a pen pal program, the teacher has overall expectations of learning outcomes — knowledge of content, language skills, and attitudes about communication. A variety of formal and informal assessment methods can be used, depending on the students and the program.

The content of pen pal programs is determined by current events and the pen pals' locations and ages. Some of the content will be learned as a class — where the pen pals live, some history and geography, special notes about the lifestyle, and a bit about the weather. Some of what students learn will be individual and will include pen pals' preferences, families, and aspirations. Discussions and informal inventories can be useful in assessing the general knowledge about geography, history, environmental science, sports, or recreation the students have gained during their year in the program.

Students demonstrate improved language skills when their letters become longer and more detailed. Their folders function as portfolios of their work and reveal the development of their skills in a variety of areas. The transfer of new vocabulary may also be apparent in oral and written work, such as public speaking or journals.

Positive attitudes of respect and caring are evident in the way students participate in the program and convey their feelings to others. Their commitment and level of motivation are revealed in how they conduct their correspondence and in the length and tone of their letters. Students who have developed a sense of ownership in the exchange act as if they really know their pen pals and are eager to share their pen pal experience.

A Sample Time Line — A Year at a Glance

Because the school year goes by so fast and there are many other activities that demand attention, a time line makes it easier to give pen pal tasks top priority. It is helpful to know when information packages are to go out and not leave things to chance. The time line can also be used to note when information packages are mailed out and received, list descriptions of package contents, and write in extra projects and extensions.

The sample pen pal time line, complete with descriptions of the noted items, was developed collaboratively by the teachers concerned. It illustrates the joint implementation of organizational and curriculum planning during a school year by two Grade Two teachers and their classes. The teachers were introduced by the principal. When he relocated to the West Coast, he put them in touch with one another.

Along with the time line is a description of how this program was set up and maintained. The general progression from August to June in this time line is typical, yet there is still room for creativity and flexibility in content and approach.

Sample Pen Pal Timeline

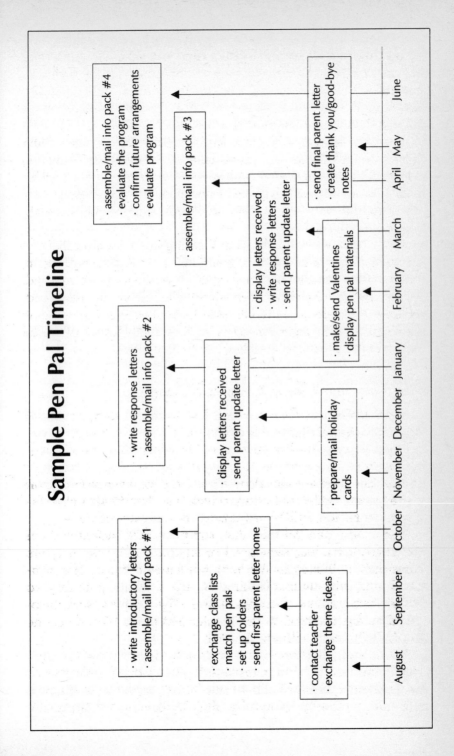

August — September — October — November — December — January — February — March — April — May — June

September box:
- contact teacher
- exchange theme ideas

October box:
- exchange class lists
- match pen pals
- set up folders
- send first parent letter home

- write introductory letters
- assemble/mail info pack #1

December box:
- prepare/mail holiday cards

January box:
- display letters received
- send parent update letter

- write response letters
- assemble/mail info pack #2

February box:
- make/send Valentines
- display pen pal materials

March box:
- display letters received
- write response letters
- send parent update letter

- assemble/mail info pack #3

May box:
- send final parent letter
- create thank you/good-bye notes

- assemble/mail info pack #4
- evaluate the program
- confirm future arrangements
- evaluate program

Although this exchange was between two primary grade class-rooms, the ideas are transferable to other levels.

August

Even though they had been in touch in June, one of the teachers decided to make contact with her counterpart on the West Coast before the school year started. In her experience, things often change over the summer — teachers sometimes are reassigned, change their minds, decide to take courses which increase their work load, or are faced with unforeseeable family or health concerns. She did not want to leave anything to chance and figured that if something had happened to change her counterpart's mind, there would still be time to make other arrangements. The teacher was pleased she had obtained both the home and school addresses and telephone numbers in the spring to be sure her pen pal colleague could be reached ahead of time.

At this point she did not have her class list, but she knew the approximate number of boys and girls she would have and the social studies curriculum she planned to teach as she and the teacher librarian collaboratively planned the units — apples, ice and snow, and communities. When she got in touch, she discovered that the other teacher did communities, ice and snow, and space. They decided to share dates of birthdays and construct bulletin board graphs of the combined classes. During the second term, they could exchange newspaper weather information for their ice and snow unit because of differing climates. Throughout the year to enrich their community studies, they would gather and share information about their respective cities.

September

When she arrived at school on the first day, the pen pal list from her partner on the West Coast was waiting for her in the office. She immediately set to work to match the list with her own in order to create the pen pal pairs. She decided on a random match which seemed fair and which also avoided the necessity of designing a selection process for students she did not know. Because she had fewer students than her partner teacher, she assigned a boy and girl to one of her students whom she felt could handle the extra task. She felt that this match would remain in place for the year, unless the numbers changed in either class, in which case they would have to adapt.

Her next step was to set up pen pal folders with two pockets — one for working copies sent, and the other for letters received. She prepared copies of a label template, to be completed by each student with the pen pal's name and school address. The label was then attached to one of the pockets, and the students decorated the front and back of their folders with maps and postcards related to their locations.

Once the children were settled in, she sent a letter home to parents to let them know that a pen pal program was being implemented and how they could lend support.

October

To get students started on their introductory letter, the home teacher handed out a pattern letter.

Hi! Let me introduce myself.

My name is

_____ .

I am _____ years old.

My birthday is on

_____

The people in my family are: _____ _____

_____ _____ _____

My pets are _____ _____

Here are some of my favourites:

Colour _____ Food _____

T.V. Show _____ Subject _____

Sport _____ Book _____

Each child took the pattern letter home in the pen pal folder, along with a note from the teacher requesting a recent photograph of the child, and completed the letter with the help of a family member. Before sending out the letters, the teacher made sure that all the students had included the date of their birthday, as the other class would need the information for their graph. The children used their own data to start constructing a birthday picture graph on the class bulletin board. They were so excited that they kept asking when they would have their pen pals' birthdays to finish the graph. The teacher decided that she had better assemble and mail, as quickly as possible, the initial information package containing her cover letter, a picture of the school, a school newsletter, a postcard of the city, the children's letters, photographs, and leaf rubbings.

November

This month, the students prepared holiday cards to send to their pen pals. The teacher mailed them in a separate package in plenty of time. The arrival of their first pen pal package created a stir. It contained computerized introductory letters, as shown on pages 79-80. Clipped to the letters were photographs of their pen pals wearing hats depicting what they wanted to be when they grew up. Her partner teacher had also included a map of their city and marked the location of their school.

The children were thrilled and keen to read their letters to one another. They immediately wanted to use the dates of their pen pals' birthdays to finish their graph, but at the same time the photographs captured their imagination. They tried guessing what their pen pals wanted to be without looking at the labels on the back of the photos. When the flurry of activity calmed down, they also pored over the map, pointing out street names that were similar to those in their own city. This paved the way for a mini-lesson on mapping and street names, and the children followed this up by creating individual maps of their neighborhood.

December

The introductory letters were placed in the pen pal folders and taken home, along with a family update letter that invited family members to come in to see the display and the children's birthday graph. When all the materials were returned, the

My name is <u>Christopher</u>. My birthday

is on <u>August 14</u>. I am <u>6</u> years old.

In my family, there are <u>4</u> people and <u>1</u> pet.

I have <u>1</u> brother and <u>0</u> sisters. Here is a

picture of my family.

My best friend's name is <u>David</u>.

My favourite food is <u>chicken</u>. My

favourite T.V. show is <u>YTV</u>.

When I grow up I want to be a <u>policeman</u>.

Here is a picture of my favourite <u>toy</u>.

teacher created a bulletin board display in the school's front hallway for viewing.

January

When they returned from holiday, the children reread their introductory letters to refresh their memories. Because they were Grade Two students and this was to be an original letter, not a patterned response, the teacher took them through the process of brainstorming to help them ask relevant questions and respond to information their pen pals provided. She put up two large pieces of chart paper on the board — one labelled **Things We Could Tell Our Pen Pals**, and the other called **Things We Could Ask Our Pen Pals**. (See page 82.) The children's ideas were listed on the charts for reference as they composed their working copies in class.

After proofreading and editing their working copies with the teacher's help, the students wrote their neat copies on decorated paper. For both copies, they were encouraged to follow **Working Copy** and **Neat Copy Guideline Sheets**, which they kept in their folders. (See page 83.)

When all the children had completed their letters and brought in newspaper articles about the recent winter storm they had experienced, the teacher assembled and mailed her second information package. This one contained a cover letter, the pen pal letters, the class collection of newspaper articles, and a new school-produced calendar featuring student art.

February

As part of their language arts program, the children composed Valentine rhymes to use on greeting cards for their pen pals. The teacher sent these in a special Valentine's Day package to her partner teacher and class. Later in the month they received their second package from the West Coast, which included a week's worth of weather maps from the local paper along with the letters.

The letters went home for the children to share with their families. A note from the teacher placed in each folder provided the following tips for response:

- find out what your child already knows about his or her pen pal

Things We Could Tell Our Pen Pals

- answers to their questions

- our Valentine's Day

- our Arctic legends

- skating lessons finished

- all about March Break

- what we want to be when we grow up

- our favorites

Things We Could Ask Our Pen Pals

- their favorites

- about their March Break

- about their family

- about their class work

- about school events

- about the weather in British Columbia

Working Copy Guideline Sheet

1. Reread the last letter you received to remember what your pen pal wrote.

2. Reread the lists we came up with about what we could *tell* and *ask* our pen pals.

3. Think of all the ideas you will put in your letter.

4. Write down your ideas.

5. Spell the words the best you can.

6. Write about two pages.

7. Ask a friend to proofread your letter for you.

Neat Copy Guideline Sheet

1. Reread your working copy.

2. Pay attention to the proofreading suggestions.

3. Copy the letter and all the corrections on the special paper.

4. Reread your neat copy. Make sure it is *neat* and *correct*.

- listen to your child read the letter
- rehearse possible answers to questions posed in the letter
- discuss other personal information which could be passed on
- share the enthusiasm

A few students kept right on top of the standings of the hockey team in their pen pals' city. Others were interested in how much warmer it is in British Columbia than here and continued to make weather comparisons on their own.

March

When all the letters from the latest pen pal exchange were returned from home, the teacher created a special pen pal display in the classroom. By now the students were aware of the process of writing a response, so the brainstorming session went smoothly. It generated many ideas which were copied from the chart paper by the class recorder for insertion into each child's folder.

Drawing on the current ideas list and using the working copy guideline sheets, students composed their response letters. The children read their letters and made some preliminary corrections with partners; then the teacher assisted in proofreading and editing once again. She felt the children were ready to write their neat copies at home. The working copy, the Guideline Sheet, and special paper were taken home in their folders, along with another letter to update families on the pen pal exchanges.

April

The children's finished letters were brought back to school, and the teacher assembled and mailed her third information package. Along with the letters, she included a copy of their class newsletter and the follow-up activity from a math unit — spring flower pictures made from geometrical paper shapes. With the end of the year rapidly approaching, it was difficult to predict when their last letters would arrive and whether or not there would be enough time to respond. She decided the students could create thank-you and good-bye cards for the fourth and final package, which would be sent in June. In this way, their correspondence would not be dependent upon the arrival of the pen pal package.

May

The teacher prepared small country maps to resemble post cards which the children used to write short notes in class saying a few final words to their pen pals. The children felt sad at having to say good-bye so early and hoped that they would receive a letter before the end of school. The teacher crossed her fingers and assured them they would receive at least a card. Some were already asking if they could keep writing during the summer, and even next year, when they realized that they and their pen pals would be in a different grade.

The teacher sent home a final family update letter to highlight the year's activities and bring the program to a close. Remembering the children's comments, she also requested that families who wanted to encourage continuing correspondence over the summer permit their children to share their home addresses with their pen pals.

June

Gathering the final good-bye postcards, the teacher checked the accuracy of the home addresses for those who wished to continue corresponding. She included the school yearbook and a cover letter in which she expressed her satisfaction with the program and her desire to continue the pen pal connection for the coming school year. She also mentioned several suggestions to improve the timing of communications, especially since the students had not had a chance to respond to a letter in their last note.

A few days before school ended and the children were to take their pen pal folders home, they were pleasantly surprised to see a familiar envelope from the West Coast. Their pen pals had been delighted to receive the good-bye letters and promises to continue the correspondence. The teacher realized that this would be the last time many of them would hear from one another, but she sincerely hoped a few would continue to write.

It was amazing to see the way the children reacted to the program. Everyone was able to handle the volume of writing, including Stephanie, with her two pen pals, who might have been overwhelmed by it all. I often heard pen pal comments spilling over into other conversations and in their dictated comments for our class newsletter.

Sometimes I even saw related vocabulary being written in the children's journals.

With all the interest that the pen pal program generated, I'm really glad that we brought it in. I hope that, next year, my pen pal partner in British Columbia will want to do it again.

Exchange Visits — Face to Face

In many cases, including the pen pal program just described, the distances between schools prohibit exchange visits. When the schools are in neighboring communities, however, it is a worthwhile addition to the program to arrange pen pal exchange visits between the classes. The following shows the experience of one pair of classes.

In our initial planning session, my pen pal teacher and I decided to arrange an exchange visit in the spring since our schools were about an hour's drive apart. We developed an exchange visit checklist (as shown on page 87) in anticipation of the required planning.

As the time drew nearer, the dates and details were confirmed in a letter to families. The students prepared by brainstorming what they would say and do during the visit, and they anticipated the event in their journals.

The visit was worth all the planning. When it was over, I focussed on preparations for the other class to visit us. To prepare the students for their role as hosts, we discussed the items on the **Pen Pal Visit Information Sheet** shown on pages 88-89. The topics were chosen to help them feel comfortable conversing with friends whom they knew mainly through letters. The students completed the sheet at home and returned it to school on the day of the visit.

We had a busy time showing our visitors around the school and our neighborhood. Halfway though the afternoon when they retraced their steps to their own school, my class recorded the day for their scrapbooks.

Several days later, we received thank-you letters from our visitors. This was the last of our correspondence. As shown on page 90, some of them were printed by hand, while others were produced by computer.

Exchange Visit Checklist
Hosting a Visit

Visiting teacher and class

Before

____ decide on date and times of visit

____ confirm visit with administration

____ send initial letter to parents

____ contact parent volunteers

____ plan itinerary

____ contact any outside sources/locations regarding itinerary

____ send itinerary and map to visiting teacher

____ make snack/lunch arrangements

____ make contingency plans in case of inclement weather

____ send update letter to parents

____ make invitations for visitors

____ send invitations to visitors

____ review itinerary

____ discuss and complete pen pal visit information sheet

____ send reminder to parents before the visit

____ pick up the snacks/lunch

After

____ record the event in picture and story

____ send thank-you notes to parent volunteers

Pen Pal Visit Information Sheet

Date:

Three things about me I can tell are:

_____

_____

_____

_____

_____

_____

Three things about my class I can show are:

_____

_____

_____

_____

_____

_____

Three things about our school I can show are:

_____

_____

_____

_____

_____

_____

Pen Pal Visit Information Sheet (2)

Three ways I can be helpful and friendly are:

_____

_____

_____

_____

_____

_____

_____

Here is my complete home address for my pen pal. Then we can keep in touch during the summer and maybe even next year.

_____

_____

_____

_____

_____

_____

_____

Be sure to do this on another sheet of paper if you have a second pen pal to give your address to.

Dear Robbie this is the last time I will be writing to you and I am geting a swimming pool in June. I am very very excited. In every house that I have lived in, I have had a pool. and I allso mite be going away for a few days. What are you doing for the Summer? Tell me in your letter. I had a great time when you came here. I enjoyed writing to you this year.Goodbye.

From Jessica

June 4

Dear Tanya

Thank you for the visit. It was fun.
I liked the tour arond the school. We
hade a nice rade to your school. We went
on a bas, subway and a street car. I
liked Riverdale farm. I saw pigs, ducks.
and more. At lunch I liked the food. I liked
the picnic. It was fun. I liked makeing
the candles. And the paper was fun
too.

from Karen

Teacher Journal Entry

June 15

Another busy year has zipped by. The pen pal program was one of the most interesting ones I've done and the e-mail added a whole new dimension. Corina's off-and-on-again problems with her computers were not expected, but I guess when you add technology you have to accept the bugs and all. We certainly had our share.

But all the problems were well worth it. When the e-mail worked, the kids looked forward to getting their messages on-screen and sharing them with each other. However, the surprise package from Corina's class was the bee's knees. Who would have thought they'd send us a video? The kids were delighted, because even though they had exchanged photos earlier in the year, seeing their pen pals in action gave them a whole new perspective of their friends. Gosh, I wished I'd thought of it. Corina didn't tell me — she wanted it to be a surprise. It was. I'll have to think of something to spring on her class next year.

4 / Twinning

September 23

Wow! Now what have I gotten myself into? Drew's mom picked up on our twinning program in a big way. She wants to bring in an artist, wants to spearhead a Celebrate Jamaica day in the spring, wants I don't know what else! She's from Trinidad and still goes down there every year to help with Carnival. She loves our Caribbean connection and wants the kids to experience it, too. She's even lined up an artist who's into "mas-making." May be able to get her to help with costumes through an artist-in-the-schools program. Will need to get a proposal ready.

December 11

Guess who dropped in with more tropical fruit for the class? You guessed it, Drew's mom. Last month it was sugar cane and before that mangoes. Wonder what it'll be next? Cassava? Anyway the kids enjoy whatever she brings. I've seen papayas and mangoes in the stores, but I wonder where on earth she found the guavas. The kids couldn't get over the humongous seed in the mango. A few of them wanted to plant it so we're giving it a try. Drew's mom took a few minutes to fill in the forms before she zipped off. Looks like the artist'll be here for a week of preparation and the Friday of the parade.

April 17

Great news! Our proposal's been accepted. The artist can come in ahead of time to show us her Carnival slides. They'll love it, judging from the way they pore over my huge book on carnivals. It's the heaviest one in my Carib collection, but they still lug it home. Have a bunch of parents lined up for promotion, decorations, playground setup, and parade. Yesterday after school was our first meeting, and they're really into this event. Better remember to send letters home to let everyone else know what's happening and get them to come. Need more parents to help with photography, booths, refreshments, make-up, and costumes that morning. Need a letter for all the teachers too — so their classes can join in. Wonder how to display those beautiful drawings of fruit and wildlife from that last info package from Jamaica.

May 24

Had the most perfect day for our Celebrate Jamaica day, warm and sunny. Costumes were spectacular — waves, butterflies, parrots, and flowers. Had a pretty good crowd, lots of classes in the yard for our jump-up. Were they ever glad to have a chance to wear summer clothes for a change. I'm amazed at the decorations Kyle's mom did — how simple yet effective those colored streamers were, blowing among the trees. They looked like rainbow snakes. My kids — I was so proud of them — sounded great singing their Calypso song with Madame — trust her to find a spot for our twinning in her French program. The dancing was infectious and the kids all had a turn showing off for the crowd. A local reporter actually came — nice to know our news release worked. Can't wait to see his article. Saw Jenny's mom taking loads of photos. Can't wait to see them, either.

Twinning Partnerships

Twinning partnerships connect a classroom in one school with a classroom in another school anywhere in the world. These connections extend beyond the exchanges of letters and information packages of pen pal programs.

World travellers who get to know people in other lands reach a broader understanding of the places they have visited than do casual tourists who take superficial tours of the same locales. Feelings of mutual respect and goodwill are fostered as people from two cultures get together. In the same way, when two classes from different schools or even from different countries are twinned and exchange information, all participants are enriched as they get to know one another and represent their culture to the other group.

Twinning programs encourage students to develop global perspectives and better understandings of other cultures. Students in one school examine their own surroundings, values, and lifestyles in order to describe and compare themselves to their twin. Twinning is a way to create communication links between different societies.

For teachers as well as students, twinning is an enriching experience. Teachers derive personal satisfaction from corresponding with colleagues of the twinned classes. Their exchanges by regular mail, telephone, or e-mail cover topics ranging from professional development to teaching conditions. It is insightful to compare and contrast qualifications and policy within their respective countries.

Reaching Out

For the most part, teachers need to be creative and assertive in finding like-minded colleagues who are prepared to enter a twinning relationship. On the one hand, they are keen to offer their students contact beyond their own country; on the other, they lack international channels of communication, even though some countries may have formal programs to match classes through a central organization. For these reasons, informal networks and a **Teacher Information Sheet**, such as that found on page 14, are essential for making initial contacts with possible twinning partners.

In addition to the educational resources mentioned in Chapter 3, "Pen Pals and Cyberpals," teachers can try making contact through the following:

- consulates and embassies
- tourists agencies and boards
- chambers of commerce
- ethnic organizations
- university language departments

They can also draw on contacts that are made as they themselves or their friends and colleagues go travelling.

Names, addresses, and telephone numbers of the departments of education of particular countries may be obtained through their official diplomatic representatives here. Many countries have a public relations component to their tourist industry which can provide information about educational institutions. Likewise, many cities have community organizations, such as Chambers of Commerce, which represent businesses and may have lists of schools on file for the areas they promote. When they are travelling in foreign countries, teachers can plan to visit schools to become acquainted with principals and teachers who may have an interest in twinning. Here at home, many ethnic and cultural groups maintain links with their countries of origin through ethnic organizations and clubs. These groups may be able to refer the names of individuals who have direct or indirect connections to schools in their former countries. Instructors and professors of foreign languages at colleges and universities can often suggest the names of colleagues in countries abroad. Frequently, they travel to the country of their language specialization and are knowledgeable about the people and their surroundings.

When setting up a twinning program, classes are matched on the basis of the age and grade level of the students concerned. National language, geographic location, and special interests are also possible factors in selecting a suitable twin. For example, if a Grade Five class in North America were studying rain forests, their teacher might look for a class of ten- and eleven-year-olds in a tropical country. An extra dimension would be added if the class in North America had knowledge of Spanish and the twin was located in a Spanish-speaking country.

Organizational Planning

After persevering to develop a connection and making the commitment to become twinned, teachers can start to develop some preliminary plans for the school year. Some of the things to consider and to begin working on are the following:

- writing the initial letter
- frequency of exchanges
- the medium of exchange
- using twinning program folders
- preparing information packages
- mailing and receiving packages
- involving families

Writing the Initial Letter

As in personal relationships, the first contact often has the greatest impact and affects the future tone of the communications. As the two teachers set up their program, ideally before the school year begins, they introduce themselves, their school, and their classes to one another. Although letters are the usual mode of communication, e-mail is becoming popular.

In their initial exchange of letters, twinned teachers can have a frank discussion about the resources that will be available to the twinning program and make some decisions about the content and frequency of the information packages that will be sent over the course of the school year. Because access to equipment and consumable resources varies greatly and will affect the program, it is essential to exchange this information right at the outset.

Dear Ms Girand,

In reply to the letter from Debra Dennis Development Education Officer, I am pleased to inform you that our request has been granted for our continued twinning.

I am still teaching Grade 2 but with a new set of 59 children-between the ages of 6 and 7. Grade 2 consists of 258 children in 5 Grades.

School was opened for the Christmas Term on September 7 with 1,568 children and 28 teachers including the principal on staff.

There is no computer at our school. We would be very grateful for the audio cassette tape.

We can communicate with you about our Jamaican food, money and people's occupation. Later on you will be informed about the other topics.

Below you will find the names of 4 children who you can match penpals with.

I do hope that this year will be a very interesting and educative one.

Sincerely yours,
Ronjel

For instance, it will be necessary to determine carefully and sensitively whether basic school supplies are readily available in both classrooms. The twinned teacher may have access to pencils and note paper, but the school system may not provide other materials, such as chart paper, construction paper, or markers. In addition, teachers may want to investigate their respective resource centres for equipment, such as tape recorders, film projectors, video players, cameras, computers, and photo-copiers, in order to incorporate them into the program.

Establishing the Frequency of Exchanges

How frequently the exchanges of information packages take place will depend on the participating schools' resources and administrative support, teachers' schedules and commitment, as well as students' grade and skill levels. To maintain a reasonably consistent program, at least two packages should be exchanged in the course of the school year. Other than the basic correspondence, most items are sent by air mail, and so delivery times may affect how often parcels are sent.

Deciding on the Medium of Exchange

Until recently, handwritten or typewritten letters have been the chief medium of exchange in twinning programs, with other items, such as posters, maps, flags, and newspapers, included in packages sent by regular mail. But today, twinned class communication can take additional forms. Telephone calls add a personal touch to a program, and electronic mail adds immediacy. Today's classes can take advantage of both systems by conducting e-mail dialogue and mailing information packages.

Using Twinning Program Folders

As described in Chapter 3, "Pen Pals and Cyberpals," individual student folders are useful for organizing all materials relating to the twinning program. Throughout the year, folders can be taken home and the contents shared. With a heightened awareness of their twinned class's country, students want to collect other items, such as newspaper and magazine articles, book reviews, pamphlets, and postcards. These can be placed in their folders along with materials they receive in the information packages from their twinned class. By the end of the year, students will have amassed unique collections which are meaningful to them.

Preparing Information Packages

A main focus of a twinning program is the process of preparing information packages to share. To begin, students discuss and list topics and questions that they want to investigate, such as familiar cultural observances that may be of interest to the twinned class. After making a selection from their list, they undertake research individually, in pairs, or in small groups, drawing information about the different topics from various sources, such as newspapers, encyclopedias, and interviews. Students then organize and synthesize the text and pictures into a pleasing format, perhaps with an overall theme. As symbols of friendship, students can include small, personal objects which convey something about themselves and their school.

Mailing and Receiving Packages

Finished information packages are sent to the twinned class as soon as possible to allow for delivery time. Because of time constraints, packages should be sent by air mail wherever possible. Although less expensive, surface mail may take months to reach its destination, interrupting the necessary exchanges in the twinning program.

Tips for Mailing Parcels

Consult the post office for rates and regulations regarding parcels sent to the twinned country.

Comply with customs regulations concerning vegetables, plants, and animal matter.

Wrap packages securely following post office rules.

Address parcels clearly and include a return address.

Label packages "N.C.V." — No Commercial Value — and "Printed Matter — Educational Material Only."

Insist on using stamps of different values which are collectible instead of using postage labels.

Declare packages as gifts, and complete the customs declaration forms.

Notify the twinned teacher that a parcel has been sent.

When time is not crucial, however, surface mail is an economical way to mail heavy parcels, such as those containing donated books. The following are some tips for mailing parcels.

Involving Families

Many families will enthusiastically support and contribute to the twinning program in their child's classroom. They may be able to assist with making the initial contact and encourage their child to contribute to the information packages that are being sent to the twin. Some families may be persuaded to help with the costs of mailings or to gather books or other resources for sharing with the twinned class.

Introductory letters sent home at the beginning of the school year can set out the background of the program, the class's expectations for it, and how the family can help. Update letters keep families informed, especially about information packages, whose contents can be sent home to share. In the update letters, families can also be invited to view displays and attend special events. Articles in school newsletters throughout the year can keep the family informed about the program as well. A letter at the end of the school year can touch on program highlights and, generally, bring closure to it.

Curriculum Planning

Detailed planning, based on available resources and the curriculum, ensures the success of the twinning program. Such planning involves consideration of the following:

- subject area or theme focus
- curriculum integration
- identifying appropriate initiating activities
- deciding what kinds of information to exchange
- gathering resources
- preparing other materials
- program extensions
- program assessment

Sample Twinning Project Web

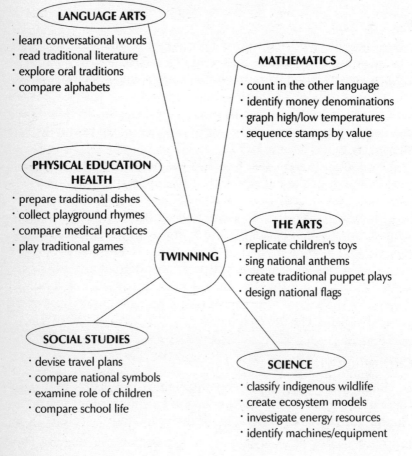

LANGUAGE ARTS
- learn conversational words
- read traditional literature
- explore oral traditions
- compare alphabets

MATHEMATICS
- count in the other language
- identify money denominations
- graph high/low temperatures
- sequence stamps by value

PHYSICAL EDUCATION HEALTH
- prepare traditional dishes
- collect playground rhymes
- compare medical practices
- play traditional games

THE ARTS
- replicate children's toys
- sing national anthems
- create traditional puppet plays
- design national flags

TWINNING

SOCIAL STUDIES
- devise travel plans
- compare national symbols
- examine role of children
- compare school life

SCIENCE
- classify indigenous wildlife
- create ecosystem models
- investigate energy resources
- identify machines/equipment

Subject Area or Theme Focus

By their nature, twinning programs emphasize social studies. Much of what can be learned about the respective countries falls into three categories — where we live, who we are, and how we live. Within the first category, information about geography, environment, and housing are characteristic; in the second, history, culture, beliefs, art, and laws; and in the third, food, work, play, communication, and school. In fact, it is possible to integrate every subject area within the curriculum in some way, as shown in the **Twinning Project Web** in this chapter.

Curriculum Integration

Twinning is a teaching approach in which teachers are facilitators and students are active participants who ask relevant questions, organize research, analyze information, and make decisions. Their exchanges reflect their attitudes and values because they communicate what is important to them, including their own hopes and concerns for the future.

Twinning is beneficial in a number of ways. It provides personal glimpses into the lives and customs of other cultures. Students learn how to collect, organize, and present information effectively, and then compare their end products with those of their twins. Teachers find that twinning creates an enriched learning environment in which activities can be integrated into the curriculum and be used to improve students' composition skills. This is especially applicable when students are studying a second language.

Using a web assists in identifying cross-curricular connections that can be made through a twinning program. (There is a blank web on page 102 and a sample filled-in web on page 103.)

Although social studies is the main subject area of study, the process of getting to know one's own country — and that of a new friend — can involve all areas of the curriculum. Once teachers familiarize themselves with their twinned class's country, they can record possible curriculum connections on a subject area web.

By creating webs such as this, teachers have a general reference point throughout the year to guide them in making connections whenever possible. For example, keeping the web in mind, a teacher developed the following subject area activities throughout the year.

LANGUAGE ARTS

The teacher created a class library on a Caribbean theme using her own books, as well as many from the school and public libraries. Selections of fiction and non-fiction were read to the class on a regular basis. Students had opportunities to read the books at school and at home. They kept track of the books they

Twinning Topic Question Web

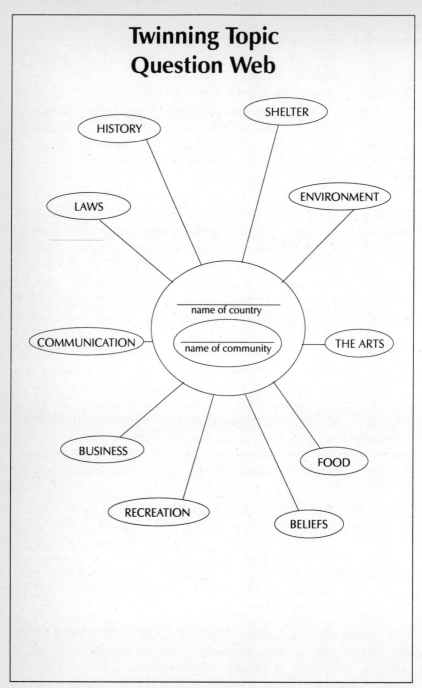

- SHELTER
- HISTORY
- ENVIRONMENT
- LAWS
- name of country
- name of community
- COMMUNICATION
- THE ARTS
- BUSINESS
- FOOD
- RECREATION
- BELIEFS

St. Lucia Curriculum Connections

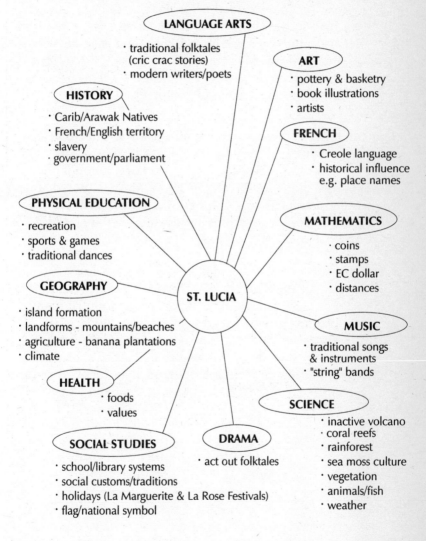

LANGUAGE ARTS
· traditional folktales
  (cric crac stories)
· modern writers/poets

ART
· pottery & basketry
· book illustrations
· artists

HISTORY
· Carib/Arawak Natives
· French/English territory
· slavery
· government/parliament

FRENCH
· Creole language
· historical influence
  e.g. place names

PHYSICAL EDUCATION
· recreation
· sports & games
· traditional dances

MATHEMATICS
· coins
· stamps
· EC dollar
· distances

GEOGRAPHY
· island formation
· landforms - mountains/beaches
· agriculture - banana plantations
· climate

ST. LUCIA

MUSIC
· traditional songs
  & instruments
· "string" bands

HEALTH
· foods
· values

SCIENCE
· inactive volcano
· coral reefs
· rainforest
· sea moss culture
· vegetation
· animals/fish
· weather

SOCIAL STUDIES
· school/library systems
· social customs/traditions
· holidays (La Marguerite & La Rose Festivals)
· flag/national symbol

DRAMA
· act out folktales

read by using student-created Caribbean passports in which they recorded titles, authors, and illustrators. The teacher stamped their passports each time an entry was made.

HEALTH

During the year the teacher highlighted tropical foods by teaching mini-lessons. Sometimes the food items were mentioned in stories which were read to the class. Other times, entries were found in her tropical fruit and vegetable guide book and in a cookbook. Samples of the foods were categorized by food groups, passed around, and eaten. From this direct experience, students drew pictures and wrote short descriptions of each item.

SCIENCE

During the winter, the teacher organized an activity that contrasted the weather in the home country and that of the twin. Her students brought newspaper weather charts to school. They located a major city in each of the two countries, noted their daily high temperatures, and graphed them for two weeks. Discussions centred around interpreting the data on the graph.

MATH

Stamps from the parcels were collected and used for a money activity in the spring. The teacher mounted single stamps on cardboard and placed them in a box. Home country stamps were treated the same way. Magnifiers were included in the kit because she knew her students enjoyed examining the beautiful, intricate designs. She made the kit available in class. The students also took it home to complete activities, such as identifying the cost of the stamps, comparing their values, and seriating them.

MULTICULTURALISM

Teachers who use twinning as a jumping-off point for multicultural studies find that exploring a country is an exhilarating experience. The awareness that we all come from different races and cultures fosters an understanding of our commonality on this shared planet. Most important, learning about other countries through twinning helps children realize that there is a world beyond them and that what is right, safe, and comfortable should be the same for all. Better decision-making in the future will depend on such an understanding.

Identifying Appropriate Initiating Activities

When the new school year resumes, initiating activities lay the groundwork for the twinning program. Regardless of their age, students come to their new grade with a range of exposures to the concept of their own and others' countries. Some have had no opportunity to travel within their own country and do not understand how people in the world are organized. Others have developed a sense of the nation in which they live and have travelled extensively. With such a range, knowing the students helps to determine which activities are appropriate and will meet their needs. Initiating activities can help to establish what students already know and move them to thinking about what they do not know but want to find out.

The following are some possible initiating activities.

What We Know; What We Want To Find Out

One simple way to begin is through a brainstorming activity in which students list whatever they already know and what they want to find out about their twin. The following excerpts are from lists generated by a class twinned with one in the Caribbean.

What we know...	*What we want to find out...*
• grow oranges, carrots, mangoes	• do they have cats and dogs?
• lots of sun	• what do they like to eat?
• no winter	• do they have any bikes?
• coconut palms	• what are the schools like?
• beaches and ocean	• are there a lot of farms?

Know Your Countries?

This initiating activity is adaptable to different grade levels.

Begin with brainstorming sessions in small groups, each with its own recorder and reporter. Students think of all the countries they know by drawing on their prior knowledge from relatives, travel, reading, and current events. While observing the groups, teachers can use the inquiry method to ensure that their own country and the twin's country are included. When the time is up, each reporter reads the groups' lists while the teacher and the rest of the class use chart paper or the board to sort the names into categories — provinces or states, cities, countries, continents, and other.

In the lower grades, place names that are not countries, such as cities and continents, are frequently mentioned. Sorting helps younger students distinguish one from another. In the upper grades, the sorting process may require fewer categories.

After Know Your Countries? has been completed as the first step, students might participate in one of these three follow-up activities to extend their understanding.

What's Our Flag?

Once the home country and twinned country have been highlighted on the countries list, the national flags of both are introduced. As a hands-on activity, the children make flags of the two countries. Particular attention can be drawn to the colors, shapes, and designs involved. Older students might investigate the origins and historical significance of the flags. The twin country's flags are used as decorations for the class's twinning folders. The class's own flags are sent to the twinned class's school in the first information package. Students gain an appreciation of flags as symbols that represent nations.

Where Is It?

Information about each of the locations of the home class and twinned class is placed on a diagram representing the world. Starting with the home class's school in the centre circle, a series of concentric circles is added, one at a time. Then the name of the class's city, state or province, country, continent, hemisphere, and, finally, planet are inserted. The same sequence is followed for the twinned class's school. By looking at both diagrams, interesting observations can be made about which circles are distinct for each class and which are common. Older students might be challenged to develop other visual organizers, such as Venn diagrams, to show the overlapping areas.

> ## Zig-Zag Map
>
> The countries from the list provide students with destinations to travel around the world. They locate and identify countries on a wall map or globe. By locating the countries in the order in which they are listed, students randomly move on the map. In the process, they traverse such features as bodies of water, continents, mountain ranges, the equator, tropics, and meridians. The journey can be tracked with pins and colored yarn. Students gain a greater sense of where countries, including those of both twinned classes, are situated relative to one another, and they begin to develop global awareness.

Deciding What Kinds of Information to Exchange

Any information that increases student knowledge and understanding of the way others live is suitable for exchanging. Students find it fascinating to compare package contents that have been developed by peers from their respective cultures. Initial exchanges generally include personal introductions, school descriptions, and community overviews, all of which come directly from the students' experiences.

Introductory letters, such as those used in Chapter 3, simply require students to look to their own families and preferences for the contents. Whether conveyed by pictures or words, this basic information establishes rapport with the twinned class, as shown in the work on page 108 from two students in the Caribbean.

Gathering Resources

Students' own schools are ready-made topics for them to begin their research. They can supply details about the following to describe their school to their twinned class:

- number of students in class and school
- number of teachers in school
- length of the school day and year
- subjects studied
- playground games
- important school rules
- transportation to and from school
- favorite things about school
- things they would change about school and why

Just as research about their schools relies on their personal experiences, so, too, does their initial investigation of their community, but in less detail. To start with, they create an overview of their community, leaving the in-depth investigation for further study. Their focus is on aspects of the community they encounter every day, and they might mention several of the following:

- their houses and streets
- local transportation
- shops and businesses
- nearby land forms (lakes or mountains)
- entertainment and recreation

As students continue to explore their community, they come to realize that it is built from and by people who share a place, a time, and a way of life. Their previous knowledge becomes significant when seen in this new light, while new discoveries are meaningful and lend excitement. The outcome of their exploration motivates them to use drawings, photographs, poetry, maps, and songs to make their community come alive for their twinned class.

Subsequent packages thus may include information on topics that students develop as they learn more fully about their own community.

To begin their exploration, students can be encouraged to discuss, as a class or in small groups, the categories found in the **Twinning Topic Question Web** on page 110. Through discussion, questions are formulated, recorded, and displayed for the class to view.

As shown in this example, some of the resulting questions could then lead to topics for students to research and present as reports, pictures, charts, and graphs. When these end products are received by the twinned class, they are valuable because they constitute authentic, first-hand information about a different city or country.

Students can use a chart with two columns labelled **Home Community** and **Twinned Community** to organize their thoughts. In the left-hand column are categories such as those in the **Twinning Topic Question Web**. Students complete the chart with the information both researched and received, which

Sample Twinning Topic
Question Web

SHELTER
· How are our homes suited to our climate?
· What are our important buildings?

HISTORY
· Where did our ancestors come from?
· Who are our heroes?

ENVIRONMENT
· What is our weather like?
· What are our wild animals and birds like?

LAWS
· Who makes the laws?
· Who keeps the peace?

OUR COUNTRY
OUR COMMUNITY

COMMUNICATION
· What languages do we speak?
· How do we get our news?

THE ARTS
· What kind of music do we enjoy?
· What are our most famous works of art?

BUSINESS
· What are the kinds of jobs in our community?
· What is our currency and how is it produced?

FOOD
· What are our main foods?
· Where does our food come from?

RECREATION
· How do we spend our fun time?
· What popular sports do we watch?

BELIEFS
· What are our major religions?
· How are festival days celebrated?

reveals the similarities and differences between communities for each category.

Since making comparisons of information exchanged on the same topics is one of the main focusses of a twinning program, teachers can ensure that this will be possible by planning ahead of time. One way is to agree on a predetermined list of topics, with students in both classes making selections from the same list. Another way is to give one class the responsibility for selecting the topics for both. In this case, the recipients follow the lead of their twinned class's topic research.

If the twinned teachers have synchronized their topics, then students will have many bases for comparisons. In the examples on pages 112-113, two twinned students researched wildlife in their respective countries.

Preparing Other Materials

In addition to sending project research that the students themselves have done, many kinds of related resource materials can be included in information packages. For instance, if the transportation system is one of the topics of comparison, then sending a copy of the local transit system map provides first-hand information. Sharing resources may also include sending the necessary tape recorder to accompany an audio-tape of city sounds, a particularly well illustrated book of native legends along with the students' report on that topic, or coins for a mathematics unit on money. Other resources might include inexpensive or free items, such as the following:

- brochures and posters (tourist, museum, business, and art gallery)
- calendars
- magazines and catalogues
- post cards and photographs
- newspaper articles
- hand-made objects (animal models)
- bookmarks, stickers, buttons, and pins
- items with national symbols (pencils, erasers, and flags)

Program Extensions

Spontaneous opportunities, in terms of people and resources, enable classes to try something new and different, as in the case

Grizzly Bears

Grizzly Bears Belong to the same Family as the Brown Bears.
They can grow up to 8 Feet Long and weieh 800 pounds. The colour of their coat can be from creamy brown to almost Black their limbs are Black and the fur of many grizzlies is tipped with white. They are also called silver tips. They have sharp curved claws.
By camilla

A Grizzly Bear By camilla

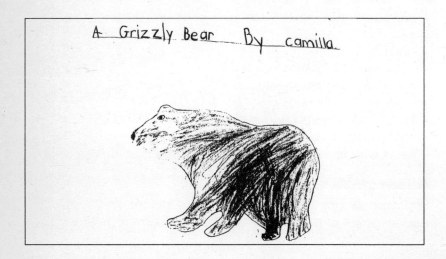

An Alligator

Kamla

This is an alligator. It is a reptile. It is found in Jamaica but not as much as in other foreign countres It is a very dangerous animal. It eats its food whole. It also eats human being. It lives mostly in muddy waters. It has scales but no fins. If you see an alligator run for your life.

of the Grade Twos' Celebrate Jamaica day described at the beginning of the chapter.

Additional activities related to the twinned country might include the following:

- invite a storyteller versed in the country's lore
- attend a musical, dance, or dramatic performance
- gather oral traditional stories on tape or video
- create musical instruments and artifacts

Program Assessment

Just as in the assessment of pen pal programs discussed in the previous chapter, teachers need to consider the twinning program's content and the learning outcomes they anticipate for their students in order to determine the effectiveness of the program. During the school year, students will have learned about their country and their twinned class's country in a social studies context. Therefore, assessment discussions and inventories would focus on the knowledge they acquired individually and collectively concerning geography, history, culture, and lifestyle.

Students can be encouraged to revisit early questions they had about their twin in order to assess for themselves the new information they have and the gaps in their knowledge they have filled.

The skills that are developed throughout the year are dependent upon the type of activities in which students have participated. They might have used various thinking skills in an inquiry approach or practical, hands-on activities with concrete materials and equipment. Records of students' research or finished products, if not the items themselves, are available in their twinned folders for review and evaluation.

Along with the content and skills developed through a twinning program, attitudes start to undergo changes over the course of the year. Students become informed about differences and develop tolerance and a global perspective. They can be encouraged to reflect on whether communication with others has helped them understand more about themselves in their community. They can ask themselves whether it has encouraged or enriched their commitment to a more sustainable and peaceful future. An important aspect of assessment may hinge on whether the class enjoyed the twinning process, as shown in

Dear Jacob,

It was nice being your friend. We learnt some things about Canada. We hope you learnt some about St. Lucia too. Have a happy holiday It is now time to say good bye. from Jacqueline

Dear Ms. Girard,

This is our last and final package to you. Enclosed you will find some writings, letters and art work. There is a photograph of my students and myself. I am in on aqua blue dress with a cosage. This picture was taken on Teacher's Day in my classroom. Some other members of staff are in the picture.

I sent you some samples of Jamaican shells and you did not mention about them. Let me hope that if you did not get them before, you will receive them by now. They were sent about a week after the lost package was sent.

My year of twinning has been a very interesting and rewarding one. My students enjoyed the twinning exercise. immensely and especially the correspondence with their penpals. They felt so proud getting their own letters.

I too will be unable to continue the twinning exercise. I will be going off to college for a one year Diploma Course commencing in September.

I have introduced one of my Grade 2 stad teachers to the twinning exercise and she has consented. I do hope her correspondence will be as enjoyable as ours.

Let me wish for you success in your educational endeavours. May God continue to guide, keep and bless you.

Yours sincerely,
Ronjel Smith

Sample Twinning Timeline

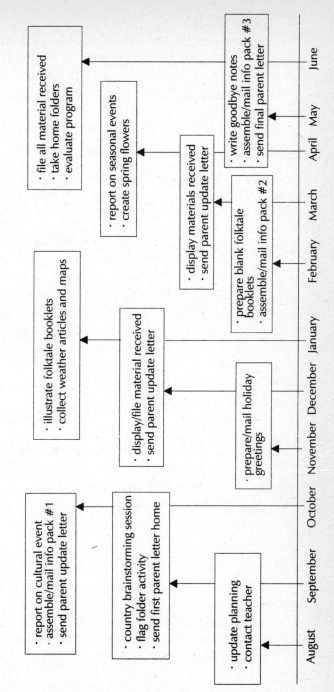

August
- update planning
- contact teacher

September
- country brainstorming session
- flag folder activity
- send first parent letter home

October
- report on cultural event
- assemble/mail info pack #1
- send parent update letter

November
- prepare/mail holiday greetings

December
- display/file material received
- send parent update letter

January
- illustrate folktale booklets
- collect weather articles and maps

February
- prepare blank folktale booklets
- assemble/mail info pack #2

March
- display materials received
- send parent update letter

April
- report on seasonal events
- create spring flowers

May
- write goodbye notes
- assemble/mail info pack #3
- send final parent letter

June
- file all material received
- take home folders
- evaluate program

one student's final letter to the twinned school in Canada. (See page 115.)

In retrospect, teachers might ask themselves whether they would participate in a twinning program again and express their reasons, along with a summarized evaluation, to their twinned teacher, such as the letter on page 116, which accompanied a final information package.

A Sample Time Line — A Year at a Glance

In addition to their previously cited organizational advantages, time lines are particularly useful to co-ordinate the mailing of information packages, an integral part of twinning programs. Long-term planning ensures that projects are started early enough, sometimes out of season, in order to be received on time.

The sample time line, complete with descriptions of the noted items, is similar to one followed by a Grade Three Canadian teacher and her Stage Three St. Lucian counterpart during the sixth year of their twinning program. Their original contact had been through the Canadian Teachers' Federation's former School Twinning Program. Still following many of its original guidelines, they were now in the midst of a creation of their own, an indigenous publishing project.

August

Having agreed in June to continue their successful format from the previous year, the two teachers exchanged personal letters over the summer. They outlined their plans to each other and described the students they were anticipating.

September

The Grade Three teacher began early in the school year to raise the awareness level of her class to different countries around the world through a variety of social studies activities. Attention was focussed on St. Lucia, and the symbolism of its flag was discussed. Students then replicated it on the cover of their folders, which were taken home for the first time with a letter explaining the program to their families.

October

In previous years, the teachers had discovered that Halloween was not celebrated in St. Lucia, but the La Marguerite flower festival occurred in the same month. They thought students would enjoy sharing and comparing information about the these two cultural events. The home teacher prepared the first information package, which contained introductory messages, a chart story about Halloween in Canada, drawings of each child in costume, and a pack of Halloween stickers. Parents were informed of the students' efforts.

November

The first week of the month found the students busily creating holiday greetings with glitter and cotton balls. The cards were sent along with contributions of the craft materials they had enjoyed using.

December

The class was excited when the first information package arrived bearing an array of exotic stamps. The contents revealed a chart story about the twinned class's school celebration of their La Marguerite festival, a cassette tape of the children singing traditional songs, and drawings of the costumed participants. The home teacher typed and copied the story for each student's folder to be shared at home, along with the pictures and a parent update letter providing background information on flower festivals and next term's focus.

January

Students illustrated their own copies of St. Lucian folk tales which had been recounted by their twinned class's teacher. They shared their results in a partner reader session — reading their stories aloud to each other. Throughout the month, students became acquainted with the range of information they could glean from weather articles and newspapers.

February

The home teacher produced a class set of folk tale booklets for the twinned teacher to distribute to her students. The booklets and some packages of crayons were part of the second information package. A collection of weather articles and maps was sent so that the twinned class could contrast their climate with a northern one. A picture book about animals in winter and drawings of the students engaged in winter sports rounded out the theme.

March

The second information package received from the twinned class contained colorful pictures and stories about the flora and fauna of the island. There were hand-made Easter cards for everyone in the class and tiny shells collected by the students during their families' Sunday visits to the beach. The cards and shells were shown to their best advantage in a display in the school foyer. The update letter sent home this time invited parents to visit the school to view this tropical display.

April

Signs of spring were everywhere when the home class collaborated on a seasonal chart story and decorated it with pictures cut from seed catalogues. As an ongoing project, students used construction, tissue, and crepe papers to create spring flowers, which were labelled with their names.

May

The spring chart story and paper flowers were assembled for mailing. The third information package also contained notes in which students expressed their thanks, shared their thoughts, and said good-bye. The final parent letter summarized the year's program and included student comments.

June

As the twinning program came to a close, the bulletin board display was dismantled. All materials were distributed amongst the students and placed in their folders to be taken home to keep. The class discussed the good things about the program and the aspects which could have been improved. Their ideas became part of the evaluation process, along with parents' comments and both teachers' reflections.

Twinning Projects as Joint Endeavors

In addition to brief, individual subject area activities, longer projects can incorporate many subject areas and enhance the twinning program. Joint twinning projects are collaboratively planned and implemented by the teachers who have a number of factors to consider when making long-distance arrangements. Exchanging information through postal systems is time-consuming and may be expensive. Telephone charges may be prohibitive in some cases. It is possible to get bogged down going through normal bureaucratic channels. In spite of these limitations, a school year is long enough to accomplish joint projects. The following projects — Computer Communication Link-up with Barbados and St. Lucian Folk Tale Publishing — show what is possible when involving students in meaningful endeavors beyond their classrooms.

Computer Communication Link-up with Barbados

The Computer Communication Link-up with Barbados project was part of an anti-racist education plan with a technology component at Earlscourt Public School, Toronto, Canada. The aim of the project was to offer the school and community an opportunity for racial understanding in a real context. In addition to regular mail, computer technology was used to expand the learning environment beyond the classroom and help Canadian and Barbadian students work together to learn about each other.

The project involved twinning a Grade Five-Six Canadian class with peers at Cuthbert Moore Primary School, St. George, Barbados. Students began the project by exchanging letters of introduction that included questions about lifestyles, industries, education, government, and weather. When they knew they would be asked similar questions in return, students were motivated to learn more about their own country.

Students were busy researching both countries and eager to make a direct connection with their twinned class when the telephone line was finally installed in February. The electronic bulletin board was established, and its use increased the students' desire for more personal interaction. By the end of the month, a plan to visit their twinned class was in place. Subsequently, the school and community worked together to make the students' dream a reality.

At the end of May, a group of students, teachers, and parents travelled to Barbados. At the welcoming and farewell ceremonies they sang their national anthems and school songs and exchanged flags, books, gifts, and hugs. During their week-long stay they visited Cuthbert Moore Primary School, where they were involved in computer, science, sports, and environmental activities. As well, they toured historical points of interest to experience the culture and heritage of the island.

The special project in their twinned program was beneficial not only to all those who participated directly but also to those who were indirectly involved. In learning more about themselves and their peers in Barbados, students became more aware of their Canadian identity. They demonstrated positive attitudes toward members of their twinned class through working and playing together. The joint fund-raising efforts by the school and local businesses heightened students' community awareness. As a result, they became better representatives of their school and looked forward to hosting a reciprocal visit in the future.

St. Lucian Folk Tale Publishing

Mangoes and Maple is an indigenous publishing project that is part of the twinning program between Montcrest School, Canada, and Babonneau Infant School, St. Lucia. Its purpose is to transform St. Lucian stories from the oral tradition to student-illustrated picture books. These stories provide opportunities for students to make personal connections with one aspect of the St. Lucian culture. Given their own copies of the stories in printed form, students from both countries are cast in the role of illustrators and respond creatively to the text.

As part of their correspondence, the twinned teachers exchange information and stories about their cultures. According to the twinned teacher in St. Lucia, the story "Thin Legs, Big Belly, and Large Mouth" is an integral part of their oral tradition. "This is a story every St. Lucian child knows. This is the first story a mother relates to her child. This she does as soon as the child can understand. It is related in Creole to children in the rural areas."

When the Canadian teacher discovered it was nowhere to be found in print to share with her students, she wanted to capture the story in black and white.

The two teachers discussed and planned the possibilities of taking the story from its original form and transforming it into a meaningful written end product for both classes. It was decided that the twinned teacher would write an English version of the story, and the home teacher would use it to produce the text in spiral-bound booklets for all the students to illustrate.

After she received the story, the home teacher read it and blocked the text so that the story was divided into chunks that could be illustrated. She designed text for the front cover and wrote the introduction for each school. The pages were photocopied, assembled, and bound. A class set and a few extras were sent in the information package to St. Lucia, to be completed by the students there based on their first-hand knowledge of the story.

Meanwhile, students in Canada learned more about the St. Lucian culture before they received their copies of the story. Because the story featured paw paws, or papayas, this fruit became the focus of a mini-lesson similar to the ones mentioned in the Health activity in this chapter. Once they knew what the paw paw tree looked like and had experienced the attributes of the papaya fruit, the students began their illustrations. Their completed books were shared in class and at home. An extra copy was donated to the school library and another was exchanged with the twinned school, to the delight of all concerned.

Teacher Journal Entry

June 30

It's still hard to believe how our twinning program took off this year. One minute we were sending intro letters to a class in the Caribbean and the next thing I knew we had a bit of the Caribbean right under our noses. Just shows what a few motivated types can do! The school's response was fantastic — guess everyone relates to music and celebration. It may have taken extra planning, paperwork, and phoning, but it was sure worth a fling with the new and different. After all, that's what it's all about.

Professional Resources

Ahmad, N. 1996. *CyberSurfer: The OWL Internet Guide for Kids.* Toronto, ON: OWL Books.

Anderson, C.C., Nicklas, S.K., and Crawford, A.R. 1994. *Global Understandings: A Framework for Teaching and Learning.* Alexandria, VA: Association for Supervision and Curriculum Development.

Bianconi, S. "Adopt a Grandparent." 1995. *FWTAO Newsletter.* 14(1), September/October.

Brown, J. *Flat Stanley.* 1964. New York, NY: Harper & Row.

Cameron, C., Politano, C., and Morris, D. 1989. *Buddies: Collaborative Learning Through Shared Experience.* Vancouver, BC: Creative Curriculum.

Carletti, S., Girard, S., and Willing, K.R. 1991. *The Library/Classroom Connection.* Markham, ON: Pembroke Publishers, and Portsmouth, NH: Heinemann.

Carletti, S., Girard, S., and Willing, K.R. 1993. *Sign Out Science: Simple Hands-on Experiments Using Everyday Materials.* Markham, ON: Pembroke Publishers, 1993.

Classroom Connect: The K-12 Educators' Practical Guide to Using the Internet and Commercial Online Services. Wentworth Worldwide Media, Inc. 1866 Colonial Village Lane, Lancaster, PA 17605.

Developmental Studies Center. 1994. *At Home in our Schools: A Guide to Schoolwide Activities that Build Community.* Oakland, CA: Developmental Studies Center.

Educational Leadership: Connecting with the Community and the World of Work. 1995. 52(8), May. Alexandra, VA: Association for Supervision and Curriculum Development.

Friends Forever Pen Pals. Park West Station, P.O. Box 20103, New York, NY 10025.

Green Teacher: The Planet Society. 1996. 48, June. Toronto, ON.

Green Teacher: Twinning Schools on a Small Planet. 1994. 37, February/March. Toronto, ON.

Hoban, L. 1976. *Arthur's Pen Pal.* New York, NY: Harper-Collins.

International Youth Service. Laaksonen & Pirkkala. Kristiinank, 5B Turku. Postal address: PO Box 125, Fin-20101, Turku, Finland.

James, E. and Barkin, C. 1993. *Sincerely Yours: How to Write Great Letters.* New York, NY: Clarion.

Learning: Successful Teaching Today. "Reader Exchange." The Education Center, Greensboro, NC.

Lewis, B.A. 1995. *The Kids' Guide to Service Projects.* Minneapolis, MN: Free Spirit Publishing.

Martin, A.M. 1990. *Karen's Grandmothers.* New York, NY: Scholastic.

Martin, A.M. 1992. *Karen's Pen Pal.* New York, NY: Scholastic.

Owen, T., Owston, R., and Dickie, C. 1995. *The Learning Highway.* Toronto, ON: Key Porter Books.

Parsons, L. *Response Journals.* 1990. Markham, ON: Pembroke Publishers, and Portsmouth, NH: Heinemann.

Pedersen, T. and Moss, F. 1995. *Internet for Kids: A Beginner's Guide to Surfing the Net.* New York, NY: Price Stern Sloan.

The Planet Society. (A program of the United Nations Educational, Scientific & Cultural Organization, or UNESCO.) *See Green Teacher* 48. Toronto, ON.

Student Letter Exchange. Waseca, MN 56093. Internet address is http://www.pen_pal.com/

Willing, K.R. and Girard, S. 1990. *Learning Together: Computer-Integrated Classrooms. Markham, ON: Pembroke Publishers.*

World Pen Pals. International Institute of Minnesota. 1694 Como Ave., St. Paul, MN 55108.

Wyeth, S.D. 1989. *P.S. Forget It! (Pen Pals: Book Three).* New York, NY: Dell.

Index